NEPALI
MIGRANT
WOMEN

Gender and Globalization

Susan S. Wadley, *Series Editor*

Other titles in the Gender and Globalization series

*Bodies That Remember: Women's Indigenous Knowledge
and Cosmopolitanism in South Asian Poetry*
    Anita Anantharam
Imperial Citizen: Marriage and Citizenship in the Ottoman Frontier Provinces of Iraq
    Karen M. Kern
Jamaat-e-Islami Women in Pakistan: Vanguard of a New Modernity?
    Amina Jamal
*Modernizing Marriage: Family, Ideology, and Law in Nineteenth- and
Early Twentieth-Century Egypt*
    Kenneth M. Cuno
The Moroccan Women's Rights Movement
    Amy Young Evrard
*Super Girls, Gangstas, Freeters, and Xenomaniacs: Gender and Modernity
in Global Youth Culture*
    Susan Dewey and Karen J. Brison, eds.
Women, Insecurity, and Violence in a Post-9/11 World
    Bronwyn Winter
Women, Islam, and Identity: Public Life in Private Spaces in Uzbekistan
    Svetlana Peshkova

For a full list of titles in this series, visit https://press.syr.edu/
supressbook-series/gender-and-globalization/.

NEPALI
Migrant Women

o   o   o

Resistance and Survival in America

Shobha Hamal Gurung

Foreword by Dorothy E. Smith

Syracuse University Press

First Paperback Edition 2021
21 22 23 24 25 26   6 5 4 3 2 1

∞ The paper used in this publication meets the minimum requirements of the
American National Standard for Information Sciences—Permanence of Paper for
Printed Library Materials, ANSI Z39.48-1992.

For a listing of books published and distributed by Syracuse University Press,
visit https://press.syr.edu.

ISBN: 978-0-8156-3712-7 (paperback)   978-0-8156-3413-3 (hardcover)
          978-0-8156-5347-9 (e-book)

Library of Congress has cataloged the hardcover edition as follows:

Gurung, Shobha, author.
    Nepali migrant women : resistance and survival in America / Shobha Hamal
Gurung ; foreword by Dorothy E. Smith. — First edition.
        pages cm. — (Gender and globalization)
    Includes bibliographical references and index.
    ISBN 978-0-8156-3413-3 (cloth : alk. paper) — ISBN 978-0-8156-5347-9 (e-book)
1. Nepali people—United States—Social conditions.   2. Nepali people—United
States—Economic conditions.   3. Women immigrants—United States—Social
conditions.   4. Women immigrants—United States—Economic conditions.
5. Transnationalism.   6. Nepal—Emigration and immigration—Social aspects.
7. United States—Emigration and immigration—Social aspects.   I. Title.
    E184.S69G87 2015
        305.8914'95073—dc23   2015028642

Manufactured in the United States of America

For my loving parents,
Luxmi Devi and Shamsher Dhoj Hamal,
and for all the women who made this book possible.

o   o   o

Contents

Foreword, DOROTHY E. SMITH   *ix*

Acknowledgments   *xi*

1. Coming to America
   Gendered Labor, Women's Agency, and Transnationalism   1

2. Nepali Women Coming to America
   Why and How?   22

3. The Informal Economic World
   Shifting Roles, Experiences, and Identities   46

4. Informal Economic Work
   Delusions, Challenges, and Contradictions   58

5. Shifting Gender Roles in Private and Public Domains
   Immigration, Migration, and Transnational Family Dynamics   84

6. Transnational Community Building
   Ties, Connections, and Practices   113

7. Conclusion
   From Informal Workers to Transnational Community Builders   140

Appendix: *Research Participants' Demographic
           and Socioeconomic Backgrounds*   155

Glossary   159

Works Cited   161

Index   173

o　o　o

Foreword

THOUGH I'M A SOCIOLOGIST I bring no specialized academic background
to my reading of Shobha Hamal Gurung's book about Nepalese women
immigrants working in low-paid domestic or other service work settings
in the United States. As I read, I began to realize how much her book does
to undo the ordinary public stereotyping of immigrant workers in Western
countries. I had taken for granted that they come primarily seeking economic advantage and to escape serious problems of poverty in their home
countries. Shobha Hamal Gurung has remade my understanding. As she
explores with Nepalese women immigrants in Boston and New York their
work, family, and community connections, we learn that though they are
ill-paid and work mostly in jobs that rely on the ordinary domestic skills
that women acquire in family households and as mothers, they are very
well educated and in some cases have worked in professional jobs in their
own country before emigrating.

Because rates of currency exchange favor Nepalese currency, Hamal
Gurung describes how even low wages allow the women interviewed to
give significant support to their families in Nepal. Some also contribute to
schools and other social ventures that support communities back home. She
also shows us how these immigrant workers create and build transnational
networks, partly familial but also organized among the community of Nepalese women in the United States. My own experience as an immigrant wife
of an American citizen was of a sharp and painful cutting-out of much that
had been personally meaningful in my life. But these Nepalese women,
whether or not they experienced anything of that, are creating new relations and new ways of relating that keep their connectedness active and,
indeed, allow them to look forward to returning home when they retire.

What is very special about Hamal Gurung's book is that the women she talked with never become objects of study; they are people from whom she learned a great deal that was new to her and she passes what she has learned from them on to those who read. Learning and discovery have been my experience of reading this book. I would not, of course, assume that other national groupings of immigrants in Western countries are engaged in the same transnational network building as these Nepalese women. Indeed I've learned from my reading here to stop making assumptions and allowing public stereotypes to control my own thinking. I understand now that I must wait and hear what immigrant people have to tell me about how they work and live and build new connections both with their distant homes and with other immigrants from the same region. I have learned also to recognize the presence of such underlying networks as an important modification of the isolating purity that some nations seek to preserve. Yes, on the one hand, in the making of global connections among people there is the ubiquitous power of transnational capital, but also hidden and largely still unknown there are familial and other nonformal connections preserved by people who have migrated. As Hamal Gurung shows.

I write this Foreword a week or so after the terrible earthquakes that devastated Nepal. As I listen to the radio news in Canada or read Internet and newspaper articles, Hamal Gurung's work has made me conscious of the many speakers of Nepalese background in the Canadian media who are connecting us to the experiences of people in Nepal and what is needed. And then I read a news story describing how Nepalese women in New York—employed in just those kinds of domestic jobs Hamal Gurung tells us about in this book—are coming together to organize help for people in distant and now-isolated villages in Nepal. I love this book.

Dorothy E. Smith

o   o   o

Acknowledgments

THIS BOOK is rooted in the emergence of Nepali women's migration process and their transnational activism. It tells the stories of these migrant, immigrant, and nonimmigrant domestics and service workers. I owe my deepest gratitude to all the women who shared their lived experiences with me with great vision and enthusiasm. This book would not have been possible without their narratives, generosity, and insights. I am forever indebted to them for allowing me to narrate their experiences.

Many other people and institutions have supported me intellectually, financially, and technically on this book. My research interest started in early 2000 in Boston when I witnessed a migration flow of educated Nepali women and their work in the informal service sectors. Discussions about a book on the subject began during my academic position at the University of Connecticut. My conversations with South Asian, immigration and globalization, and Nepali scholars took the concept to the next level. I began research in 2005 with my colleague Bandana Purkayastha, who deserves special recognition for guiding me through the technical and initial phase. I am grateful to Bandana and Celine-Marie Pascale for their constructive feedback, persistent guidance, and encouragement, which made it possible for me to turn the research into a book.

I have also greatly benefitted from the intellectual vision, constructive feedback, and technical advice of many other scholars, friends, and colleagues. I invited Dorothy E. Smith to Southern Utah University in 2009 to deliver a keynote address for Women's Week and was able to spend a few days with her. While driving, dining, and walking in the region's national parks, she shared with me memories of her childhood and work life in the United Kingdom, and her academic, familial, and community experiences in the United States and Canada. Her stories were inspirational for examining women's work, family, and community lives. I was fortunate to discuss my research with her, particularly regarding feminist theory and ethnography. Her intellectual wisdom has informed and enriched the feminist ethnography and analysis of women's everyday lives in this book.

Mary Romero graciously agreed to read the book prospectus while she was under deadline pressure for her own book. Her comments have been extremely useful in revisiting some theories and organizing the book chapters. I have also greatly benefitted from feedback and advice from Nepali scholars including Anup Pahari, Chandra Bhadra, and Kamal Regmi, who graciously read many chapters with razor-sharp intellect. Their comments and advice on selected chapters—particularly Nepal's political economy, migration history, and gender and labor—have been instrumental. Their feedback strengthened my analysis and I deeply appreciate their input and spirited enthusiasm for this book. My friend Julia Mongo, who over the years has become my sister, has tirelessly read and edited drafts of the manuscript. Her love and humor helped me to sustain the writing process. I express my special thanks to Barret Katuna, who read various versions of the manuscript with great enthusiasm. I am grateful for her valuable editorial assistance. Jessica Cobb worked with me toward the final phase and provided constructive and thorough feedback. I am thankful to Mangesh Bhatta, Grishma Kunwar, and Shubhashis H. Gurung for transcribing and translating the interviews. Thanks also to Marita McComiskey, Jennifer Yanco, Christine Gailey, Daniel Farber, Anjana Narayan, Kathrin Zipple, Kimberly Kay Hoang, Kathryn Ratcliff, Gay Tuchman, Mercedes Santos, Cathy Scaff, Geeta Shrestha, Geeta Pfau, Bidya Ranjeet, Richard Pfau, Mala Giri, Josephine Beoku-Betts, Lorana Rivera, Gordana Rabrenovic, Luis Falcone, Margaret Abraham, Karen Kendrick, Manisha Desai, Hae Yoon Choo, Jacki Knight, Ramesh KC, Nancy Naples, Joya Mishra, Miliann Kang, Lily KC, Pradeepta Upadhyay, Wendy Wilson-Fall, Bimal Gurung, Rabindra Bhandari, Gyan Pradhan, Mary Berstein, Nahide Konak, Christine Bose, Kristy Kelly, and Daniela Jauk for their continued support. I would also like to thank Rukimini

Karki, Prem Paudyal Chhetry, and Victoria Lane for working together to create such a fantastic book cover. I am grateful to all the women who gave their valuable time and graciously agreed to be on the book cover.

During the course of researching and writing, I traveled to Boston and New York several times. My move to Utah in 2007 made these trips even more expensive. The funding that I received from the Institute for Asian American Studies at the University of Massachusetts-Boston; the Ford Foundation's Project on Low-Wage Work, Migration, and Gender; and the University of Illinois at Chicago supported my research expenses. I am thankful to these institutions, and I would like to particularly thank Paul Watanabe, Shauna Lo, Nilda Flores, Anna Guevarra, Hector Cordero, and Pallavi Banerjee for inviting me to present my research with the scholarly and activist community. I was also able to share my work at conferences and meetings that are sponsored by and connected to the following organizations: the American Sociological Association, the Society for the Study of Social Problems, Sociologists for Women in Society, UN Commission on the Status of Women 58, and the International Sociological Association. During my trip to Nepal in 2013, I also presented for the Women's Studies community at my alma mater, Padma Kanya Multiple College in Kathmandu. I would like to especially thank Chandra Bhadra, Bindu Pokharel, and other Women's Studies community members for inviting me to share my work with the students and faculty at Padma Kanya Multiple College. The comments and feedback during my conference and community presentations provided me opportunities to reflect further on my analysis and findings.

At Syracuse University Press, I would like to thank my acquisitions editor, Deanna H. McCay, for guiding me from the beginning to the final process of publishing this book. She respected my decisions about content, style, and narration. It has truly been a delight to work with Deanna. I am grateful to Susan S. Wadley, Kay Steinmetz, Mary Petrusewicz, Brendan Missett, Kelly L. Balenske, and other technical and editorial team members for their instrumental input to the publishing process.

I am also thankful to the faculty editorial board for finding the project to be an ideal fit for their series and for unanimously supporting its publication. I appreciate the amazing marketing and promotional task that Mona Hamlin undertook. I am also pleased with the anonymous reviewers who provided me with their constructive feedback. At Southern Utah University, I am thankful to my colleagues in the Department of History, Sociology, and Anthropology and Women and Gender Studies for their support. I have shared various stages of the book project with Earl Mulderink, James Aton, Emily Dean, Mark Miller, Carrie Trenholm, Rita Osborn, Michelle Orihel, Julie Simon, Danielle Dubrasky, Georgia B. Thompson, Kholoud Al-Qubbaj, and Andrew Van Alstyne. They always listened to me with great enthusiasm. Rudia Heddings and Sarah Braun warrant special recognition for their administrative assistance: Rudia took care of all the logistics, Sarah helped me receive permissions forms and crosschecked all the citations. I am grateful for their support. Some data and women's experiences in this book had been already published in the *Journal of Workplace Rights*, the University of Illinois Press, and Springer. I would like to thank all three publishers for allowing me to reuse the earlier version of that published information.

My family has been a great source of strength and inspiration throughout the research and writing of this book. I am fortunate to have such a loving and supportive family. Working on the manuscript was a laborious task, and I appreciate their patience even if some family members (my concerned parents) did not always understand why I had to work so hard during school holidays and vacations!

My brother Santosh and sister-in-law Pushpanjali welcomed me into their home in Seattle for the entire summer when I wrote the first draft. They not only cooked my favorite food everyday but also took care of all my other needs. My niece Shristi was a constant source of delight. Like my parents, she would wonder why I was going to the library and studying during my school break. My nephew Jivesh Hamal read some chapters and raised interesting questions. My brothers Gandhi and Jagdish and sisters-in-law Mona and Geeta, my sister Sofita and brother-in-law Deepak Pandey, and all my nieces and nephews provided valuable moral support from afar.

My son Shubhashis was a toddler when I began graduate work. Since then, he has been an invaluable part of my academic journey: sometimes as an observer and sometimes as a contributor. His support and patience throughout my academic life has made me persevere. He transcribed and translated all of the interviews taken during the second phase of the research for this book. During the process, he came to understand the challenges and accomplishments of migrant/immigrant communities, especially the struggles and strength of transnational mothers. I hope he takes pride in his roots and in being part of such a community.

NEPALI
MIGRANT
WOMEN

1

o   o   o

Coming to America

Gendered Labor, Women's Agency,
and Transnationalism

I work two different jobs. . . . I take care of a child and I also work in
a convenience store during weekends. . . . I have helped many women
find jobs in childcare. . . . I am also very much involved with nonprofit
organizations both in the United States and in Nepal. I help the Nepali
community organize sociocultural events and I actively participate in
fund-raising initiatives. . . . We raise money to help Nepalese both in the
United States and in Nepal.

—Childcare provider in Boston

THE VOICES of educated Nepali migrant women reflect their low-paid
work in the informal service and domestic sectors of the US economy. At
the same time, they also describe sophisticated social, cultural, and economic engagement across transnational contexts to support their families
and communities. Their stories illustrate an emerging trend in the migration stream from Nepal, a trend that defies common assumptions regarding migrant workers: educated women are increasingly migrating from
Nepal to the United States to capitalize on wage differentials to contribute
not only to their families but also to their villages and to international
charitable organizations. In doing so, they renegotiate gendered expectations regarding Nepali women's social and economic participation.

During my initial graduate study in Boston in the early 1990s, this
trend was not yet apparent. With the exception of college students, it was
unusual to hear of Nepali women migrating to the United States alone

1

without their families. The Nepali women I knew were wives of international students who had accompanied their husbands to the United States on an F2 visa (dependent of student). While the husbands studied in universities, their wives took care of the family, raised the children, and worked as skilled childcare providers for other families in their own homes. These women followed traditional Nepali gender expectations in the spheres of both home and work: they raised their families and children, supported their husbands socially and economically through graduate school, and engaged in paid care work that did not conflict with their roles as wives and mothers.

Before the mid-1990s, it was rare for Nepali married women to migrate alone to the United States to find paid work to support their family, community, and social organizations back home or to pave the way for their children and families to join them in the United States.[1] By the late 1990s, increasing numbers of Nepali migrant women were visible as workers in the informal and service sectors of Boston and New York City.[2] The majority of these women had moved or migrated to the United States alone and worked full time, particularly in service and care work. Their migration enabled them to act as the family breadwinner and provider, reversing traditional gendered migration patterns between Nepal and the United States and destabilizing traditional gendered relations in Nepali families.

Nepali migrant women's engagement in transnational activities and activism was another remarkable feature of the migrant experience that emerged in the late 1990s through which Nepali women migrants gained a new level of visibility. Migrant women's agency and leadership became apparent in local and transnational nongovernmental organizations (NGOs), social organizations, and fund-raising initiatives for

---

1. Women who migrated alone to the United States before this era were typically students. In the mid-1990s, a stream of women workers joined this stream of students.

2. In this book, the term "migrant women" refers to married, separated, or widowed women of Nepali origin, the majority of whom came to the United States alone under a variety of circumstances. Some women came for a short-term visit, some women came to attend professional seminars, and some women immigrated permanently. In chapter 2 I analyze the reasons for and durations of women's migration.

disadvantaged community members. Between 1992 and 1996, I was affiliated with and active in the Greater Boston Nepalese Community (GBNC). As a board member and adviser, I interacted closely with the local Nepalese community. Reflecting on that time, what I recall most vividly is that women (particularly in Boston) helped organize and participated in Nepali sociocultural events but did not explicitly engage in economic and political transnational activities.[3] Since then, women's agency has become central in multiple sites and multiple contexts. Nepali women are engaged in constructing Nepali identity, rebuilding a Nepali diasporic community in a transnational land, and maintaining social, economic, and political ties with their families, communities, and the home nation.

This rapid growth in single women's migration and in women's participation as the head migrants in their families and communities represents a momentous shift in Nepali migration patterns. Women's contributions of income and remittances to their families, communities, and nation have the potential to change views of migration and of gender in Nepal.[4] The migration of Nepali women to the United States also alters the US immigration landscape.[5] And Nepali women's involvement in transnational activities allows them to exercise new agency on a global stage. But what structural and personal factors compel educated women to migrate to the United States for work? How do they enter into the informal sectors of the US economy, and what kinds of labor relationships do they experience? Finally, how does Nepali women's involvement in the public sphere through paid work and transnational activities destabilize or reinforce gendered relations in Nepali families?

3. This may have been due to the small size of the Nepali community at the time and to the women's family structure.

4. This claim is applicable to only Nepali women migrants. Studies have already shown that women from many regions of Asia, particularly the Philippines and Kerala, have long migrated to the United States to support their families.

5. To capture the various intersecting statuses of women's geographical movement, I use the terms "move," "migrate," and "immigrate" interchangeably. Not all women came to the United States intending to settle permanently. Only a few of the women in this book were immigrants who came through the Diversity Visa (DV) Program.

This book addresses these questions by describing the everyday lives of Nepali migrant women. These women are not on the social or cultural radar of most people in the United States. They are rarely included in scholarly or popular writings on Asian American women, migrants/immigrants, or low-wage migrant workers. Nor are they considered as major contributors to household, national, and global economies or as transnational activists and community builders. But there are important lessons to be learned from Nepali women's experiences as migrants from Nepal, as workers in the United States, as members of transnational families, and as participants in global political and social activism. Their experiences offer insights into understudied areas of gendered labor, immigration, and transnationalism

Nepali Migrant Women: Survival and Resistance in America analyzes the unique position of Nepali women migrants to shed light on an important scholarly question on invisible female migrants and the power of their transnational engagement. It explores the lived realities of women whose economic and social contributions are vital to their households and to local, diasporic, and transnational communities. The book describes women who are simultaneously exploited workers and transnational change agents, framing these women's experiences in the context of changing local, national, and global political economies. Their experiences challenge and expand existing knowledge about gender, labor, and immigration.

As transnational migrant laborers, Nepali women's work experiences show similarities with and differences from those of other female migrant laborers in the informal economic and service sectors, including Latina and Southeast Asian female labor migrants (Chang 2000; Hondagneu-Sotelo 2007; Romero 1992). Like other migrant women workers, many Nepalis are legal migrants but undocumented workers. In contrast to other workers, however, many were also educated professionals or semiprofessionals in Nepal who now work as low-paid service or care workers in the United States. They work in arduous conditions in coethnic labor markets, yet within these markets they continue to demonstrate their agency by promoting and developing social capital in their home countries. Thus

I demonstrate that women's engagement in low-paying and exploitative work conditions is just one aspect of their lives; women rise above and beyond their work situation through their engagement with their families and with transnational communities.

Nepali women live multifaceted lives as they simultaneously engage in sociocultural, economic, and political transnationalism. I argue that women experience and broadly achieve empowerment through their leadership, agency, and commitment to making a difference for the people within their communities. In this sense, this book moves beyond the model of the victimization of Third World women in the informal labor market to show how women's engagement in transnational activism alters gendered expectations at home and abroad.

Research Context and Conceptual Frameworks

My personal biography and academic training in sociology, gender, and feminist ethnography inform this research. Like many feminist and ethnographic research agendas, this book arose from both personal and intellectual concerns. My research is rooted in years of study, work, and life in the United States as a migrant Nepali woman. Over the years, I have had opportunities to interact with Nepali immigrant, nonimmigrant, and migrant communities in various capacities, particularly through US-based Nepali organizations such as the Greater Boston Nepali Community (GBNC), the Nepali Women's Global Network (NWGN), and Help-Nepal between 1991 and 2008. In the first decade that I lived in Boston, Massachusetts, most of the Nepali women migrants I knew were well educated, middle-aged married women who performed unpaid domestic and care work at home while their husbands were workers or students in the United States. In early 2001 when I returned to Boston after completing research in Nepal, I noticed a dramatic shift in Nepali female migration, particularly in Boston and New York. Like their predecessors, many of these women were well educated and middle-aged, but instead of providing unpaid services at home, many of them worked in the informal service sector. In addition, many of these women were not "trailing wives" but instead were lone or lead migrants in their families.

The issues concerning migrant/immigrant women's lives are personal to me.[6] I am an immigrant woman, part of an emerging migrant/immigrant Nepali community and diaspora. As a member of this community, I was naturally interested in the shifting patterns of migrations taking shape around me. As a scholar, I asked: Why were these Nepali women moving or migrating alone and leaving their families behind? Why were they working in the informal service and domestic sectors when many were well educated and held professional jobs in Nepal?

Feminist scholars and researchers study the lives and experiences of women with the goal of empowerment (Fonow and Cook 1991; Collins 1991; DeVault 1999; Harding 1987; Naples 1996, 2003; Reinharz 1992; Smith 1989; Zavella 1992; Zinn 1979). My particular interest in the lives of Nepali migrant and immigrant women in the United States is related to what Smith (1989) calls the "everyday/everynight" lived experience. As a feminist ethnographer, it became my quest to investigate the circumstances under which Nepali women migrated/immigrated and to understand their work, family, and community lives—both in the United States and transnationally. My research, methodology, and conceptual framework are rooted in my own lived experience in the migrant diasporic community and my academic training in sociology, gender and feminist studies, and transnational studies.

Nepali Migrant Women builds on three main bodies of literature and scholarship: (1) studies of migration, immigration, and globalization; (2) gender, feminist, and intersectional theory; and (3) research on women's agency in a transnational context. I begin with a discussion of informal work in the service and domestic sectors and how and why migrant and immigrant women enter into such work. To contextualize women's international migration to the United States, I discuss the changing social, cultural, political, and economic landscapes in Nepal, including the women's movement in Nepal. I then move to an analysis of the dynamics of racialized gendered labor from an intersectional perspective. Next, I discuss

---

6. Over the years, my immigration status has changed from nonimmigrant F1 Student Visa to Immigrant Permanent Resident.

how changes in gender roles in private, public, and international spheres foster changes in women's positions, power, and relative autonomy. My final focus is on women's agency and the civic and humanitarian engagement through which women build transnational communities.

Globalization, Migration, and the Informal Economy

Scholars of international migration offer various explanations of people's geographical movement. The neoclassical perspective on labor migration focuses on spatial differences in labor supply and demand (Harris and Todaro 1970; Todaro 1976). Human capital theory suggests that economic inequalities and spatial disparities between areas of origin and destination tend to contribute to migrants' rational choice to move (Siddiqui 2001). Gender is missing from both of these perspectives, and women's experiences as migrants/immigrants are not included in classical migration studies (Pessar 1999).

Over the last few decades, feminist scholarship on migration/immigration has documented new trends and patterns of female international migration. Women currently make up around half the world's migrant population, and the United States attracts more female migrants than any other labor-importing nation (Pessar 1999). The restructuring of the global economy has precipitated female international migration for labor, particularly in the informal service and domestic sectors (Ward 1990; Chang 2000; Wichterich, 2000; Hondagneu-Sotelo 2007; Parreñas 2001; Ehrenreich and Hochschild 2002; Sassen 2000; Moghadam 1999, 2005). Marchand and Runyan suggest that the "feminization of labor in the context of global restructuring refers not only to the unprecedented increase in the numbers of women workers . . . but also to the flexibilization and casualization of especially women's labor to keep labor costs down and productivity up in the name of free trade, global competitiveness, and economic efficiency" (2000, 16).

In the current global economic context, informal service sector work in the Global North relies on the labor of female migrants/immigrants from the Global South. At the same time, neoliberal policies and structural adjustment programs in the developing South created unfavorable socioeconomic conditions (e.g., poverty and unemployment) that contribute to migration from that region. Thus, the global restructuring process creates the structural conditions for female international labor migration.

When explaining gendered international labor migration, the globalization literature tends to overemphasize the feminization of poverty in poor nations and the increasing demand for service and domestic workers in rich nations as motivating factors. For example, Bhadra (2007) reports the feminization of poverty as a major factor for Nepali women's labor migration in the global market. However, although women's migration is *structured* by global economic conditions, it is not *overdetermined* by these conditions; women from the Global South migrate for a number of important reasons. In this book, I illustrate the complex personal and structural factors motivating Nepali women's migration. Some women in this study came to the United States as political refugees/asylees, some came to visit friends and family members, some came for professional reasons, some came to escape gendered cultural and social oppression, and indeed some cited economic reasons as their motivation. The context for Nepali women's migration/immigration includes global economic restructuring alongside political, economic, and social changes in Nepal and a culture of gender-based exclusion and oppression.

This book illustrates how social class, education, and professional backgrounds factored into Nepali women's migration decisions and selection of a destination nation. Nepali women's international migration to the United States involved economic resources, human capital, and social capital. Applying for a visa and purchasing a plane ticket required some acumen and a great deal of money. Similarly, responding to a visa counselor at the US Embassy in Nepal to complete all the necessary paperwork at the port of entry in the United States required at least a basic level of education. Women had to understand these processes to successfully migrate.

Because this book focuses on well-educated migrant women who could navigate these processes, it contrasts with studies of the informal service and domestic sector that focus on poor and working-class female immigrants. The general image of informal, service, domestic, and care workers is that they are uneducated, unskilled, undocumented, and often from a working-class background. By examining the narratives of Nepali women, this book breaks from a monolithic view of informal migrant workers as poor women with constrained choices, showing that well-educated women may strategically take advantage of global wage and status differentials to improve their family standard of living and contribute to their communities.

Despite the varied motivations behind Nepali women's migration and despite their advantageous educational and class backgrounds, most ended up working in the informal service, domestic, and care sectors in the United States. These women worked as childcare providers, restaurant workers, housecleaners, and domestics. Hence, a significant number actually experienced downward occupational mobility. This suggests that when it comes to work in informal sectors, there are similarities in the lives of migrant women across various educational levels, social classes, and nationalities. Despite Nepali women's relatively better educational and professional backgrounds, upon migration, they also experienced "inconsistent social status in the labor market." Their experiences were similar to the cases of Filipina domestic workers reported by Parreñas (2001). Faced with a labor market segment where there is no opportunity for advancement and few opportunities to organize against exploitation, informal women workers experience deskilling, brain waste, and downward occupational mobility (Parreñas 2001; Kofman 2000).

Although female migrants engaged in informal work have gained center stage in both academic and journalistic domains, South Asian women workers in the contemporary informal economy of the United States have received very little attention, and Nepali women are barely studied at all. Although Nepali female migrants are among the fastest growing segment of the workforce in the South Asian community, particularly in informal work in major cities of the United States, they remain virtually invisible. This book helps make visible these women's lives by adding the perspectives of Nepali women migrants to feminist scholarship on labor migration and transnationalism.

Intersectionality and the Pan-Ethnic
Labor Market: Labor, Structure, and Power

Feminist sociologists and race, class, and gender scholars have employed intersectional theoretical approaches to interpret multiple marginalities and inequalities among their research subjects (Choo and Ferree

2010). For intersectional scholars, the factors of race, ethnicity, class, gender, sexuality, nationality, and citizenship status are sources of power, privilege, oppression, and marginalization, and the intersection of these factors creates a matrix of domination (Crenshaw 1991; Collins 1990; Glenn 2002; Zinn and Dill 1994). In *Making Sense of Race, Gender, and Class*, Pascale argues that "inequalities are naturalized and made meaningful through the routine production of race, gender, and class in daily life" (Pascale 2007, 18).

Taking this approach, scholars such as Rollins (1985), Glenn (1986), and Romero (1992) have examined the work lives of domestic and care workers and their exploitative work conditions in relation to women's race, class, gender, and citizenship status in the labor market. These scholars note that the US labor force has been historically stratified along race, class, and gender lines and that women of color have disproportionately shouldered domestic and reproductive labor (Glenn 1986; Romero 1992). In her classic book *Between Women: Domestics and Their Employers* (1985), Rollins reports on the growth of Caribbean and Latin American women's participation in US domestic service in the twentieth century. Referring to these women's labor conditions, Rollins states: "because of their precarious material and sometimes legal status, they are the most exploitable group within the domestic servant sector; and because they are Third World women, they will be vulnerable to the 'occupational ghettoization' European immigrant women of the nineteenth century escaped" (1985, 57).

Women from the Global South have become preferred informal sector workers, particularly in service, domestic, and care work, because their labor is cheaper and they can be easily exploited (Chang 2000; Hondagneu-Sotelo 2007; Parreñas 2001). Immigrant women who work in the domestic and care work sector are a vital workforce in the global economy, but also a disposable and vulnerable one (Chang 2000). Informal and domestic work are often unregulated and excluded from basic worker rights and legal protections. Workers without legal status are subjected to the worst work conditions and labor exploitation. Scholars have documented the exploitative labor conditions of Filipina and Latina domestic workers on the West Coast, Mexican domestic workers in the Southwest, and Caribbean domestic workers in New York (Parreñas 2001; Hondagneu-Sotelo 2007; Chang 2000; Romero 1992; Colen 1986; Sassen 2000, 2006). Das Gupta

(2008) also notes the physical, emotional, and sexual abuse in the lives of Asian women immigrants (both spousal and employer violence) in relation to their immigration status. Reflecting on the efforts of the organization Sakhi for South Asian Women to end violence against women, Das reports, "Employers underpaid and overworked their immigrant employees by threatening to expose them to immigration authorities and by impounding their passports or other identification papers" (2008, 533).[7]

My book builds on this body of scholarship to illustrate an emerging trend among South Asian women. The women I studied worked in the informal service and domestic sectors, which were segmented not only by race, class, gender, and citizenship but also by South Asian pan-ethnic affiliation. Unlike other analyses in which migrant women of color work for white families, the majority of women in my research were employed by South Asian Indian employers.[8] This book examines the work conditions and labor practices particular to employment in a pan-ethnic labor market. How does sharing a cultural background with her employer shape a woman's work experience—in terms of the benefits of comfort and the costs of vulnerability, oppression, and abuse?

The factors that made Nepali women ideal workers also produced their exploitation. Nepali women were sought out by Indian employers because of their gender, cultural backgrounds, and South Asian affiliation. These factors supported many Nepali women's preference to work for Indian employers as well. However, these factors also become sources of women's labor exploitation and emotional abuse, especially when the

---

7. Sakhi for South Asian Women is a New York City-based nonprofit organization. One of its main aims is to end all forms of violence against South Asian immigrant women.

8. I use the term "South Asian" to refer to the people, cultures, and nations of South Asia as well as those of South Asian descent. For example, the term "South Asian Indian employers" refers to both Indian American employers and employers who were immigrants from India. South Asia comprises eight nations: Afghanistan, Bangladesh, Bhutan, India, Maldives, Nepal, Pakistan, and Sri Lanka. People and cultures are extremely diverse within and across these South Asian nations; however, some South Asian nations also bear remarkable social and cultural similarities. This is particularly true for India and Nepal. I will elaborate on the pan-ethnic relationship in chapter 4.

boundary between being perceived as a family member or a worker was blurred. These points of intersection thus produced contradictory effects.

I employ an intersectional framework to analyze and interpret women's experiences. But I move beyond the intersection of race, class, gender, and citizenship in the US informal labor market to the complex sociocultural and historical relationships between Nepali women workers and their pan-coethnic Indian employers that shaped their employment, work conditions, and labor relations. Das (2008) reports on the labor exploitation of Indian immigrant women domestic workers in New York whose many professional employers were coethnics and women. By adding an ethnic component to her analysis, Das offers insights into the exploitative labor relations within the coethnic labor market. Her discussion on the coethnic aspect of gendered labor is not adequate to interpret Nepali women's pan-ethnic gendered labor experiences, however. For some Nepali women, working within the pan-ethnic labor market was a rational choice. While Das's analysis mainly revolves around labor exploitation in relation to women's social class and immigration status, I analyze both advantages and disadvantages of Nepali women's work in the pan-ethnic labor market.

Shifting Gender Roles and Power Relations: Private, Public, and International Spheres

This study also illustrates how gender operates simultaneously on multiple domains and levels. *Nepali Migrant Women* illustrates how Nepali women's international migration and participation in a globalized economy has destabilized, shifted, and reversed gender roles and relations on both the personal and societal levels. Nepali women's migration to the United States changed their conjugal, familial, and community roles and lives, fundamentally altering their position, power, and relative autonomy. When these women became the main income earners in their families, their personal, social, and political lives were altered in both local and global contexts. These shifts were sometimes contradictory. Although Nepali women's narratives suggest that their economic contributions to family, community, and nation increased their self-confidence, decision-making power, and leadership roles, their voices also reflect their exploitation and vulnerability.

Scholarship on the gendered effects of globalization has often focused on the feminization of migration and the dynamics of labor and gender in the informal service sector. Feminist scholarship on migrant/immigrant women workers in the US informal service sector has particularly focused on women's labor experiences and work conditions in relation to race, class, gender, and nationality. Although feminist scholars have discussed the issues of transnational mothers and their experiences in the US domestic and care work sector (Hondagneu-Sotelo and Avila 1997), few studies have considered the ramifications of shifting gender roles in women's conjugal, familial, and community lives on a transnational level. Feminist scholars, particularly Kibria (1990) and Das (1997), have analyzed how ethnic minority immigrant women in the United States reinvent and reconfigure family lives and arrangements. Their studies, however, do not focus on transnational wives who are the head migrants and who live away from their husbands on a different continent. By examining different domains (e.g., conjugal, family, and community) of women's everyday lives in transnational contexts, this book connects the literature on globalization, migration, gender, and feminist scholarship.

Transnationalism, Women's Agency, and Empowerment

The term "transnationalism" has been defined as migratory and cross-border activity, a process by which migrant/immigrant communities maintain ties between homelands and host countries. Transnationalism involves "the processes by which immigrants forge and sustain multi-stranded social relations that link together their societies of origin and settlement" (Schiller, Basch, and Blanc-Szanton 1992, 7). The perspective of transnationalism/transnational activity I use and develop in this book is influenced by the work of Levitt (2001, 2007) and Portes (1997). Levitt focuses on transnationalism that manifests simultaneously in different arenas of migrants/immigrants' lives. As she writes, "A transnational perspective tries to look at all layers of social life simultaneously and understand how they mutually inform each other. It recognizes that some social processes happen inside nations while many others, though rooted in nations, also cross their borders" (2007, 23).

Scholars offer various explanations on why and how migrant communities engage in transnational practices. Levitt (2001) and Portes (1997) suggest that the structural forces that limit migrant/immigrant opportunities in host nations are responsible for maintaining immigrants' social, political, and economic ties with their countries of origin. "Because increasing numbers of contemporary migrants are people of color, they often experience blocked mobility, racism, and discrimination. They are not allowed to become completely 'American' even if they want to" (Levitt 2001, 20). In this context, transnational ties, connections, and practices are responses to dislocation, displacement, shifting status and identities, and structural constraints. "Transnational practices also enable migrants to recoup their sense of purpose and self-worth. Though they may feel isolated and unwelcome as immigrants, they are still treated as respected and valued members of their sending communities, a fact that also encourages their continued membership" (Levitt 2001, 20). Along these same lines, in *Negotiating Ethnicity*, Purkayastha illustrates that middle-class and affluent South Asians in the United States "negotiate multilayered ethnicity to balance their position as racialized middle-class Americans along with their complex social location within a larger transnational arena" (2005, 5).

The Nepali migrant women in this book lived in two worlds. In one world, they were informal domestic and services workers, dedicating over twelve hours a day, six days a week to labor in service of their mostly South Asian Indian employers. In the other world, they were transnational citizens, devoting a great deal of time and energy to supporting their families and communities in Nepal, sustaining a migrant community in the United States, and engaging in transnational activism/nonprofit work that spanned borders.

Nepali Migrant Women addresses the questions of how and why Nepali migrant women straddled these two worlds by examining various dimensions of women's individual, community, and organization-based practices that transcend global boundaries. The women in this book, much like the migrant/immigrant community in Levitt's *Transnational Villagers* (2001), organized groups and communities across various global boundaries, employed various channels to seek transnational belonging, constructed a sociocultural landscape in the United States, and created a Nepali community, identity, and diaspora. Within the US context, transnational participation allowed women to reclaim their lost political and social status due to their downward occupational mobility and the social and economic constraints they faced as migrants. However, this was not their only motivation for participating in transnational activities; their participation also allowed them to assert intersecting identities of gender, nationality, class, and religion.

Existing studies (Levitt 2001, 2007) of transnationalism provide a deeper understanding of why and how migrant/immigrant communities constitute and reconstitute their lives in a transnational world. However, these studies often lack a gendered analysis and overlook women's agency. For example, Levitt's research participants in *Transnational Villagers* (2001) were not differentiated by gender. Similarly, Purkayastha's *Negotiating Ethnicity* (2005) focused on middle-class and affluent South Asian groups but did not attend to gender. Although many studies track the significant sums of money transferred back to home countries, few systematically examine the trends and flow of *women's* remittances and contributions in particular. This book explicitly examines women informal workers as they remit money to Nepal to build community institutions and social capital.

This book is unique in its focus on women's agency in building transnational community at both the local and global levels. By allocating remittances and resources individually or collectively in the host country and mobilizing a community in the homeland, Nepali women actively participated in transnational practices. By building their lives and communities across nations and continents, they bound together local and transnational families and communities. And by creating moments of ethnic and cultural solidarity through the celebration of national and religious festivals, women constructed a diasporic community. Nepali women's agency was powerful and necessary in each of these arenas.[9]

---

9. In this respect, my book relates to studies by Pessar (2001), Moghadam (2005, 2007), Desai (2002, 2009), and Katuna (2012) that examine women's agency in a transnational

The book reveals women's leadership and feminist solidarity, which they employed mainly through economic transnationalism. Women's remittance patterns illustrated multiple directions and meanings in the spiritual, civic, and humanitarian aspects of their lives. Although many women sent money to their families, others also sent money to community organizations, including religious institutions and nonreligious NGOs.[10] Many women in this study sponsored orphaned and underprivileged children. Their commitment to economic support for nonfamily members, especially the marginalized community at home, illustrates their humanitarian initiative and sense of civic responsibility. Giving and supporting deprived people in their community was part of their religious and spiritual life, part of their "dharma" and "karma." Whereas the pattern of women migrants sending money home is not new, sending money regularly to support social organizations and nonfamily members in need is a new phenomenon.

By deploying their remittances and earnings in various directions, Nepali women challenged a gendered system in which men traditionally dominated the public arena through the widespread recognition of their contributions among members of their local, national, and transnational communities. Women's earnings in the United States made these gendered shifts possible. Though their pay for hours of toil in the informal economic sectors may seem meager, Nepali migrant women were able to use this money to build a transnational community and a humanitarian society. I argue that women employed US earnings and transnational ties to enact their agency; using these tools, Nepali migrant women were able to thrive and shine. The women whose narratives constitute this book transcended their limited work environments in both the personal and professional domains and on national and transnational levels. Through

---

context. As in previous works by Kabeer (2002), Das (1997), Yuvul-Davis (1997), and Pessar (2001), this book also challenges and departs from the victimization model of the "Third World" woman.

10. As Levitt (2001) found, economic support and remittances are a vital source through which women actively participate in the cultural, social, economic, and political arenas.

their stories, this book provides insight into the gendered nature of transnational activism.

Research Methodology: Subjects, Settings, and Social and Transnational Ties

This book is based on an ethnographic study of thirty-five Nepali women workers aged twenty-eight to fifty-seven living and working in Boston and New York City. Women were selected to participate in the study based on their ethnicity, their migrant status, and their employment in the informal service and domestic sectors. The research sites were selected purposefully. New York City has the highest Nepali migrant/immigrant population in the United States and continuously attracts new migrants/immigrants because of transnational social ties. The metropolis of New York City is also a hub for informal sector work, which is often accessed through coethnic social networks. In New England, Boston attracts migrants/immigrants because of its academic and medical centers, efficient public transportation system, and close proximity to New York. Many Nepali migrants/immigrants have relatives and friends in both New York City and Boston, and they frequently move between the two cities.

I am very familiar with Boston and New York City, which gave me an advantage in developing networks with the women migrants whose voices make up this book. I have been a part of the Nepali communities in these cities for many years. Boston in particular was my academic home for more than a decade. In both cities, I lived amid the migration influx of Nepali women. I was thus able to use my personal contacts and social networks to identify research participants.

Prior to my fieldwork, I visited Boston and New York City a few times to meet with my acquaintances, some of whom already worked in the informal service and domestic sectors. Through this network, I then selected two key informants from each city with whom I discussed my research project in detail. My key informants then became my local contact point, introducing me to other women workers. They hosted a small informal lunch gathering at their homes and invited me to meet other women workers. Each of these women referred me to other women workers, and the newly referred women in turn referred me to other women. I built rapport with women mainly through phone conversations and in-person visits. Many women worked twelve hours a day, seven days a week, and they did not have much time to socialize. Thus, a phone conversation was an ideal opportunity to bond.

During my intital meeting with women, I discussed the research project with them, including the research protocol. The women often had a few questions about the purpose of the study, which I explained to them. After that, the majority enthusiastically agreed to particiapte. Because of the women's irregular work schedules and because the study involved legal immigration issues, it took a bit longer to persuade some women to participate. In such cases, I explained the research ethics and I assured their confidentiality through the use of pseudonyms. I also clarified the timing issue involved in the interview process. I told them I would conduct interviews only if and when they would be ready or available. Women felt comfortable after this conversation.

As a feminist ethnographer, I sought to understand women's experiences from their perspectives. Hence, it was important to me that the women were able to narrate their own stories. I did not interview or communicate with the women's employers. This is because it was essential to provide the women with a safe and comfortable space to share their honest lived experiences without fear of repercussions from employers or entanglements with government agencies. The women's voices are central to this book; their interpretations of their stories are the foundation of this study.

I collected information through in-depth semistructured and open-ended interviews. I also used end-of-interview questionnaires to gather information about the women's demographic profiles.[11] I collected this information in two different phases. In the first phase (2005–6), I interviewed ten women from each city. In the second phase (summer 2009), I

---

11. These various methods enabled me to analyze and triangulate data in a meaningful way.

interviewed fifteen new participants and reinterviewed five participants.[12] I conducted the interviews primarily in the Nepali language and I tape-recorded the interviews with the participants' consent. During the data analysis process, I contacted some women to clarify some of their responses.

Most of the interviews took place in the women's apartments; at their request, a few of the interviews took place in public places like parks. Whenever the interviews took place in a woman's apartment, she always shared homemade food with me. This interviewing process was possible because I am a Nepali national who shares the same first language, culture, and a similar circumstance of diasporic migration with my research participants. My status as a migrant and a mother also facilitated our conversations. As discussed by Zinn (1979), my "insider" position allowed me to access sensitive data about immigration issues and conjugal relationships through rapport building based on our shared experiences and cultural understandings. Conducting research about women's work and labor conditions, especially with these undocumented workers, would not have been possible otherwise.

As a member of the same gender, class, and ethnic community as my research participants, I had some privileges in conducting this study. I have social and religious affiliations with both the Hindu and Buddhist communities, which helped me connect with women from these two religious groups. However, my status also posed some challenges, especially when the boundaries between my Nepali migrant woman and researcher identities blurred. For example, I could not refuse lunch and dinner offers during the interviews, and some women asked about my own experience in the United States.

I am also aware of some possible limitations related to my sampling method and sample size. Although the sample size is small, the findings provide a vital exploration of emerging trends and patterns of migration

12. The second interview phase was supported by funding from the Ford Foundation and the Low Wage Work, Migration, and Gender project at the University of Illinois at Chicago.

among Nepali women, their subsequent experiences in the service and care work sectors, and how the intersections of race, class, gender, nationality, and citizenship status produce complex and sometimes contradictory effects in different domains of women's lives. Because informal work experience is the major criterion for inclusion in this study, this book is not intended to capture the work experiences of all migrant Nepali women in the United States. In a broader context, however, it provides a base from which to examine the gendered experiences and transnational lives of other educated female labor migrants who work in ethnically segmented informal labor markets.

Overview of the Book

Chapter 2 provides a historical context to understand gendered migration patterns from Nepal. I begin with a discussion of caste, class, ethnicity, gender, religion, and region in Nepal. I discuss Nepali society and its broader structural inequalities to provide readers a window into the place where Nepali women migrants began their journeys. I then discuss the women's journeys to the United States and why and under what conditions they moved or migrated or immigrated. I also provide an overview of the women's demographic and socioeconomic backgrounds and the nature of their work before and after their move. The overall discussion is vital to understanding the personal, social, cultural, political, and economic factors—including transnational networks—that shaped the international migration patterns and directions of the Nepali women migrants in this book.

Chapter 3 examines women's induction into informal service in the domestic and care work sectors. The chapter takes a close look at the factors that attract or even compel women into the informal service sector, including transnational connections and social networks, visa categories and immigration statuses, the nature of the work in the informal sector, and personal issues. The chapter discusses women's social and cultural ties and work relations with their South Asian employers in a coethnically segmented labor market that shapes the available labor opportunities. The chapter offers a gendered understanding of work within immigrant ethnic enclaves.

Chapter 4 focuses on women's work experiences. Using an intersectional framework, I examine women's work conditions and labor relations in relation to their race, class, gender, nationality, and immigration status. The chapter underscores the persistent unequal power relations between women and their employers.

In chapter 5 I examine the extent to which women have become the main earners for their families in the United States and Nepal, and the ramifications for their familial, conjugal, and community lives. The chapter focuses on shifting gender roles and relations; it illustrates how women and their husbands simultaneously confirm and subvert traditional gender roles and patriarchal ideologies. This duality, I argue, is produced by women-led migration, changing work and familial life in the postmigration/immigration United States, and the construction and deconstruction of traditional gender norms.

Chapter 6 centers on women's everyday lives in a transnational context. Women's agency and their transnational activism are the overarching themes; I show how women organize and maintain their transnational connections and ties through social, cultural, and economic activities and support. The chapter offers a window into how women develop and sustain a sense of empowerment through transnationalism and global civic engagement.

In chapter 7 I conclude by revisiting the questions, themes, major trends, and findings addressed in previous chapters. The chapter also highlights the vital roles and initiatives of local, national, and transnational-level communities and organizations in relation to women's labor, human rights issues, and women's agency and empowerment. I address the broader impact and insights drawn from these women's narratives and their policy implications.

Overall, this book offers readers insights into the lived experiences of Nepali migrant/immigrant women and connects these insights to broader issues of gendered labor, transnationalism, and women's agency and empowerment. It holds both social and sociological importance as immigration in the twenty-first century continues to grow in varied and sometimes unexpected ways.

2

○　　○　　○

Nepali Women Coming to America
Why and How?

I came to America to visit a friend. . . . Then I ended up staying here. . . .
My children and husband live in Nepal. My husband tells me that I
should pave the way to America for our family.
　　　　　　　　　　　　　　—Convenience store worker in Boston

TODAY MORE THAN EVER BEFORE, women are crossing international borders as refugees, immigrants, labor migrants, mail order brides, students,
professionals, and visitors. Women constitute approximately one-half of
all labor migrants worldwide. In some countries, such as the Philippines
and Sri Lanka, female migrants outnumber male migrants.

Migration scholars commonly consider poverty and economic neces-
sity as one of the main push factors for female international migration
and demand for female labor in the informal service sector as one of the
main pull factors. In this chapter, I place women's lived experiences at
the center of my analysis to move beyond a simple push/pull framework
based solely on global inequalites. Instead, Nepali women's voices reveal
that multiple factors at both the macro and micro levels (including personal, social, political, and transnational factors) influence Nepali wom-
en's international migration patterns and directions.

Globalization, and the economic restructuring that has accompanied
it, has accelerated the feminization of the migrant labor force. Each year,
increasing numbers of women migrate from industrializing to industri-
alized nations. These women often wind up working in the service and
domestic sectors, which are associated with traditional female work.

Nepali women are no exception to this global trend. Their migration process has coincided with major political, economic, and social changes in Nepal that began in the 1990s.

As the narratives in this chapter illustrate, local, national, and global forces combine with sociocultural factors and transnational connections and ties to shape women's migration decisions. These complex interactions must be tracked and unpacked to more fully understand who migrates, why and under what conditions, where, when, with whom, and for how long. The lives of women in this book reveal multiple reasons for female migration as well as the factors of demographics and immigration status that shape women's work choices and work conditions.

This chapter provides a background to understand the transnational lives of Nepali migrant women in the United States. I begin by giving a brief historical overview of Nepal's political economy and sociocultural landscape. A broader understanding of Nepali society is useful to contextualize individual migration decisions and to understand factors contributing to the growing flow of Nepali women migrants. Then I turn to the Nepali migrant women whose experiences are the focus of this book. This chapter answers several fundamental questions about these women: What were these women's lives like in Nepal? What multiple and intersecting factors influenced their decision to migrate? Once women decided to migrate, how did they select their destination? Finally, how did women migrate, and with whom?

Political Economy and Structural Inequalities in Nepal

The history of modern Nepal dates back to the early eighteenth century, when King Prithvi Narayan Shah initiated the process of consolidating and unifying Nepal from twenty-two various states into a single state (Hamal Gurung 2003; Pradhan 2002). The state formation process created complex and contradictory political, social, and cultural currents. King Prithvi Narayan declared Nepal "a flower garden of four *varnas* and thirty-six *jats*" and "unity in diversity" became a national slogan. However, within this garden, many non-Hindu communities experienced subjugation and oppression as the king imposed his Hindu religion on the newly unified states (Pradhan 2002). State formation further institutionalized existing forms of caste, class, ethnic, and religious stratification.[1]

Nepal continued under a monarchic system until 1846 when Prime Minister Jang Bahadur, a member of the politically and economically powerful Rana family, took power from the monarch and implemented hereditary clan-based rule. Under this system, the prime minister—always a member of the Rana family—controlled all legislative, bureaucratic, and administrative functions of the state. Jang Bahadur also promulgated the first national civil code, which subsumed all people from different castes, ethnicities, languages, and religions into one "overarching hierarchy." These groups were ranked into five different categories in a hierarchical social order (Pradhan 2002, 8). During the Rana regime (1846–1950), social, economic, and political exploitation and oppression intensified, and Nepali society became even more stratified. In terms of labor exploitation and the domination of ethnic and religious minorities, the Rana regime can be seen as a dark age in Nepal's political history (Hamal Gurung 2003).

Nepal's formal social, political, and economic dealings with the outside world began only after the overthrow of the Rana regime in 1951 when King Tribhuvan Shah returned to Nepal from exile in India and restored the monarchy. The subsequent return to absolute monarchy sidelined democracy and democratic elections for decades to come.[2] In 1962, King Tribhuvan's son, Mahendra, dissolved the popularly elected government headed by the Nepali Congress leader B. P. Koirala and imposed the uniparty Panchayat system with an absolute monarchy at its center. Under the Panchayat system, monarchs were not only the head of the state but also controlled all government, judicial, and bureaucratic functions. The stated goal of the Panchayat system was to decentralize the social, economic, and decision-making power from top to bottom along the lines

---

1. See Pradhan (2002) and Lal (2002) for further discussion of geography, geopolitics, and demographic composition in Nepal.

2. See Onta and Parajuli (2012); Basu (2010); Upadhya (2002); and Ramachandaran (2002) for a detailed discussion of key transitions in Nepal's political history (i.e., the state formation process, the Rana regime, the Panchayat system, and the democratic movement of the 1990s).

of region, caste, ethnicity, religion, and gender; in reality, this did not happen. Instead, most social, economic, and political functions remained in the royal palace, firmly within the hands of the monarchs and their kin.

The Shah monarchs were high-caste ethnic Hindus and the Nepal state was portrayed as a Hindu state. This intensified regional, caste, and ethnic-based stratification.[3] Under the Panchayat system, inequalities increased among regions and peoples of Nepal. The Nepali government adopted an economic reform policy in the mid-1980s with the goal of economic growth, unregulated labor markets, trade liberalization, and privatization of public enterprises (Hamal Gurung 2003; 2010). The implementation of neoliberal policies opened the door for a greater role of unregulated free market forces in labor, capital, and commodities.

The period between the late 1980s and 2008 witnessed significant changes in Nepal's politics and economy. In the political arena, the government changed multiple times since 1990 when Nepal transitioned from an absolute monarchy to a republican state. In response to an autocratic political system, entrenched inequalities of class, caste, and region,[4] the implementation of neoliberal polices, and a stagnating economy, an armed Maoist rebellion—also known as the "People's Movement"—began in 1996, immersing the country in a decade of civil war.[5] Political violence disrupted peace and security at the local, regional, and national levels (Hamal Gurung 2003).[6]

Part of a global wave of democratic movements in the post-Soviet era, the People's Movement aimed to realize the Nepali people's longstanding

3. See Lal (2002) and Pradhan (2002) for a detailed analysis of regional, caste, ethnic, and religious structural inequalities in a historical context.

4. According to Lawoti, citing Murshad and Gates (2005), Nepal was marked by persistent structural inequality "among different sectors: geographic regions (mountain and hills and Tarai, and east to west), rural and urban areas, and gender, ethnic and caste groups" (Lawoti 2010, 8).

5. See Lawoti's and Pahari's contributed chapters in their edited volume *The Maoist Insurgency in Nepal: Revolution in the Twenty-First Century* (2010) for the historical, social, political, and economic contexts of the Maoist insurgency.

6. Pradhan (2009) eloquently analyzes the economic fallout of the civil war.

aspirations for a democratic polity that recognized the people's civic and human rights. Structural inequalities persisted throughout the history of modern Nepal. All regimes from state formation to the Panchayat system were characterized by stratification based on caste, ethnicity, class, gender, religion, and region.[7] The Nepali people were dissatisfied with the autocratic political system, uneven economic development across the rural hinterlands and urban cities, the stagnant economy, and the state of caste, ethnic, class, gender, and religious power relations. Basu characterizes the conditions leading to the People's Movement as a "crisis of economic development, a quasi-feudal, aid-driven political structure with a nineteenth-century Hindu idiom of state formation [that] entered into a crisis of existence" (2010, 116).

Although the Communist insurgency arose with the aim of developing a casteless, classless, egalitarian, republican state, the civil war caused many Nepalis to live in constant fear, encounter violence, and lose their lives. Victims included schoolchildren, teachers, social workers, and the chief of the Nepali police force. During this period, Nepal was transformed from a state of peace to a constant state of emergency.

In spite of this violence, the People's Movement ushered in a string of social movements, including a women's movement and civil and human rights-based initiatives. The government ratified major international human rights treaties that required Nepal to adhere to the Universal Declaration of Human Rights. During this period the number of community-based Non-Governmental Organizations (NGOs) and International Non-Governmental Organizations (INGOs) grew exponentially. These NGOs and INGOs worked on a variety issues, including building physical infrastructure and advocating policies against the sex trafficking of women and girls (Shah 2002, 144). NGOs became "an alternative sector of employment for thousands of educated youths crowded out of the bloated civil service and anemic economy" (Shah 2002, 147).

---

7. Gender-based inequalities and discrimination exist across all castes/ethnicities, classes, religions, and regions. However, the nature and degree of gender inequality varies along these other lines of difference.

After immersing the country in a decade of strife, the movement was ultimately successful in restoring multiparty democracy. A second People's Movement in 2006 produced additional major political shifts in Nepal, including the overthrow of the absolute monarchy system, the institution of a multiparty democracy alongside a constitutional monarchy, and a republican state system that included a proportional electoral system with two separate constituent assemblies tasked with the writing of a new constitution for the nation. The Nepali state now guarantees fundamental human rights and equality before the law to all its citizens, regardless of caste, ethnicity, religion, or sex.

Nepali International Labor Migration in Historical Context

Throughout the country's history, Nepal's political and economic isolation, poor infrastructure, and poorly developed human capital resources affected its people's international migration patterns, their selection of destinations, and the nature of their work. Some of the oldest migration patterns involve Nepali men serving as soldiers in the British and Indian armies. These soldiers are still known as Gurkha warriors, a name derived from their origins in the hill town of Gorkha. The Gurkha troops were legendary during the nineteenth century for their achievements in the British and Indian armies.[8] Historically, international labor migration in Nepal originated as a political process. During the British Raj in India, the Rana dynasty maintained good relations with British rulers. The Rana supported the British to serve both their "personal and class interests" and the British "were happy to protect the Rana aristocracy . . . because it served their imperial design and interest, but cost them nothing" (Shrestha 1990, 81). The Ranas supplied Nepali troops to the British Army and police forces, "which prompted the British Indian government to recognize Nepal as an independent kingdom in 1923" (Basu 2010, 103).

---

8. The "brave Gurkha warriors" were renowned for their heroic fighting in World Wars I and II (Hamal Gurung 2003). See Des Chene (1991) for an in-depth discussion of the history of the Gurkha soldiers.

This relationship between Nepal and Britain established a culture of foreign employment and labor migration among Nepali men.[9] In the late nineteenth and early twentieth centuries, rural men, particularly from the Gurung, Rai, Magar, and Limbu ethnic communities in the hilly region of Nepal migrated to India and the United Kingdom to work in the army and police and remit money back home (Pahari 1991; Yamanaka 2000). In this era, international labor migration in Nepal was very limited, involving only men from specific ethnic minority groups who migrated to a specific set of jobs in only two countries.

India has long been the prime destination for Nepali labor migrants. In addition to recruiting soldiers to the British and Indian armies and police forces, India has absorbed Nepali migrants as low-paid manual laborers. India's borders to the east, west, and south of Nepal, the lack of documentation requirements for Nepali migrants, and the similarities in culture and language between the two countries attracts Nepali labor migrants on seasonal, temporary, and long-term bases. Many rural poor Nepalis, especially from the hill and mountainous regions, have sought employment on tea plantations, in the construction industry, and in restaurant and domestic sectors in the northern and northeast border regions of India.[10]

Migration in contemporary Nepal differs from previous labor migration. In the past, men migrated to India, the United Kingdom, and some Southeast Asian nations to work in both formal and informal arenas. Those who served in the British and Indian police and army forces used

9. In Nepal, the term *lahur* refers to foreign countries and the term *lahure* refers to Nepali men employed in foreign countries. In Nepal, Gurkha soldiers are usually referred to as *lahures*. For more discussion of these terms, please see Pahari (1991) and Yamanaka (2000). These authors also offer insight into the shifting international labor migration patterns of Nepalis in a historical context.

10. Nepalis have also inhabited some Indian regions, such as West Bangal, Achham, Almora, and Kumaon, for a long time. Nepali immigrants are involved in various kinds of work in India. Parts of current West Bengal, such as the district of Darjeeling, once belonged to Nepal but were exchanged for the Terai region of the current Banke district during a treaty with British India. Thus some Nepalis living in many parts of India are not immigrants but legitimate residents of those lands. Nepali women work in the tea plantations, particularly in the West Bangal region—Darjeeling, Kalimpong, and Sikkim.

formal channels to migrate and work, but many who worked in the construction industry and other manual sectors migrated and worked informally. Few Nepali people migrated to Western countries outside of the United Kingdom.

Nepal's formal social, political, and economic ties with the outside world began only in the early 1950s. The Rana regime left in its wake an underdeveloped infrastructure, a feudal, agrarian-based economy, and a mass of uneducated and unskilled citizens. During this period, people did not relocate or travel except as permitted and/or necessary. Most areas in Nepal did not have navigable roads, so getting from one place to another involved walking, sometimes for days or weeks.

After the removal of hereditary Rana premiers in the early 1950s, a spirit of nation building emerged. The first economic development plan was introduced in 1956. This plan and others that followed were concerned with infrastructure—such as the construction of paved roads—and investment in human capital. Internal migration gradually accelerated, mainly for economic opportunities. This was particularly true for the rural poor and landless people of the mountainous regions, who sought seasonal and permanent employment in lowlands and urban areas (Hamal Gurung 2003). In the 1980s, the introduction of neoliberal policies in Nepal expanded economic migration internationally. This structural change affected both the domestic economy and the labor market by increasing contact between Nepali workers and foreign markets.

Over the past twenty-five years, Nepal has joined the ranks of places in Asia like Kerala in India, Sri Lanka, Bangladesh, and the Philippines as a prime source of international labor for hire (both males and females).[11] The increased migration of Nepalis since the 1990s must be analyzed in the context of an unstable national polity, civil war, economic restructuring, unemployment, globalization, and a series of domestic political upheavals (Thieme and Wyss 2005).

The 1990 People's Movements presented a chaotic political context in which hundreds of thousands of Nepali migrants were displaced from

11. I have discussed these issues in detail in earlier articles (2003; 2010).

their homes and their livelihoods, leading to a sharp rise in both volun-
tary and forced migration. Some people migrated in search of economic
opportunities whereas many others sought to simply escape the violence
committed by both Maoist and government forces (Hamal Gurung 2003).
In this era, "the traditional flow of unskilled Nepalese to India was further
aggravated by the Maoist insurgency—with India providing an escape
for forced migrants—while labour migration to the Gulf region reached
unprecedented levels" (Bohra-Mishra 2011, 1528).

Furthermore, the People's Movement in Nepal produced "the expansion of NGOs [that] directly and indirectly contributed to the emergence
of new services and markets" (Shah 2002, 147). The proliferation of NGOs
and INGOs in Nepal brought many community leaders, international
players, professional actors, and civil and global advocacy communities
together and provided favorable conditions for global networking. This
provided a professional avenue for international migration. Connected
through various causes and organizations, Nepalis began traveling the
globe to participate in NGO forums, workshops, and conferences. These
transnational NGO networks thus added a new dimension to the international migration of Nepalis. As the World Bank reports, "Migration has
spread through networks and now involves the whole country" (2011, i).

Today, across all socioeconomic and demographic backgrounds and
regions, Nepali people are migrating globally in significant numbers and
for increasingly varied reasons. Some Nepalis migrate in search of economic opportunities and better livelihoods whereas others migrate to
escape from the political violence, threats, and insecurity. Some people
migrate for personal reasons (i.e., personal freedom and autonomy) and
yet others migrate because of their transnational connections. The trend
of Nepali people going abroad for purposes other than labor migration
(such as to study, to participate in professional training and conferences,
to permanently immigrate, to visit family and friends, or to seek political
refuge/asylum) is a recent phenomenon.

According to the World Bank's *Migration and Remittances Factbook
2011*, India, Qatar, the United States, Thailand, the United Kingdom, Saudi
Arabia, Japan, Brunei Darussalam, Australia, and Canada are the top ten
destinations for Nepali emigrants. Multiple mediating factors influence

people's reasons for migrating and their destinations. Nepalis' historical and current international migration patterns indicate that socioeconomic class is among the strongest predictors of destination. People with lower socioeconomic backgrounds tend to migrate to India, Gulf nations, and to some extent Southeast Asian nations to work in the service and domestic sectors. People from relatively higher socioeconomic backgrounds tend to migrate to the United States, Canada, Australia, and European nations for academic and professional engagement as well as to settle or work (Bohra-Mishra 2011).

The immigration/migration of Nepalis to the United States is a relatively recent phenomenon, beginning in the 1990s (Dhungel 1999).[12] Nepalis are among the fastest growing migrant communities in major US cities such as New York, Los Angeles, Washington, DC, Chicago, Dallas, and Boston. Citing the *USCIS Yearbook 2003*, Purkayastha and Ray report that "the number of Nepalis admitted [to the United States] per year ranged from 212 in 1992 to 1138 in 2002" (2010, 56). Bohra-Mishra reports that "according to the US Department of Homeland Security (2008), 83,489 Nepalis entered the US between 1998 and 2006 under the non-immigrant visa category, which mostly includes students and tourists as well as those entering the country for business and temporary work purposes" (2011, 1528).

The increasing number of Nepali students in higher education reflects this trend. According to the Institute of International Education, Nepalis represented 0.9 percent of all foreign students enrolled in US colleges and universities in the 2013–14 academic year. In terms of the number and nationality of active international students in higher education, Nepal was ranked sixteenth with 8,155 students. Given the relatively newer immigration history of Nepalis and the size of the nation, this is a remarkable trend.

---

12. Scholars have suggested various contributing factors for this trend. They include postdemocracy movements, civil war and political violence, globalization, and the USCIS-led diversity visa lottery system (Hamal Gurung 2010); democracy movements and diversity visas (Dhungel 1999); and Maoist insurgency, civil conflict, and diversity visas (Bohra-Mishra 2011).

The migration and immigration process of Nepali people to the United States must be understood in the context of the diversity visa (DV) lottery system implemented by the US Citizenship and Immigration Services (USCIS).[13] Purkayastha and Ray report, "after the amendment of the Immigration Act of 1990, Nepalis, and Bangladeshis have benefited from diversity visas, which were offered to countries that were underrepresented or had a low rate of immigration to the United States" (2010, 52). In the 2007 USCIS visa lottery, Nepal was ranked second among all thirty-two qualifying Asian countries, and 1,529 people were granted diversity visas (Bohra-Mishra 2011).

Although the Nepali population in the United States is quickly growing, Nepalis remain the smallest South Asian migrant/immigrant community in the United States. This is largely due to the relatively recent history of Nepali immigration into the United States as compared to other South Asian nationals—such as Indians, Pakistanis, Sri Lankans, and Bangladeshis.

Nepali Women's Migration to the United States

For centuries, migration within and from Nepal was the prerogative of men, but the early 1990s ushered in the growth in women's migration. Previously, women who migrated did so with or following their husbands as dependent wives. In the contemporary era, women often initiate migration, with or without their spouses and families. Historically, men in Nepal accessed nonfarm employment opportunities on a far greater scale and for much longer than women (e.g., migration for British and Indian military service). In the early 1990s, however, the industrialization of the carpet manufacturing sectors absorbed a mass of rural poor women, prompting the internal migration of Nepali women, particularly from rural to urban centers like the Kathmandu valley (Hamal Gurung 2003). The global demand for handwoven carpets created a substantial

---

13. In the late 1980s, the United States Citizenship and Immigration Services (USCIS) introduced the diversity visa (DV) lottery system with an intention to promote immigration/migration from historically "underrepresented" countries.

female factory-based wage-earning population for the first time in Nepali history (Hamal Gurung 2003).

Labor force participation by women is highest in Nepal among all South Asian countries (Institute for Social Studies Trust 2007). However, Nepali women's economic activities are invisible and their economic contributions are unrecognized at the national level. That is because the majority of women's work has remained in the low-productivity agricultural and informal economic sectors; work in these arenas is not recorded. According to the United Nations Development Programme (UNDP), the labor force participation rate is 48.9 percent for Nepali women and 67.6 percent for Nepali men (UNDP 2010). The majority of Nepali women's labor force participation is within the agricultural and informal economic sectors. The agricultural participation rate for women is 94 percent, as compared to 70 percent for men (Acharya 2000). In Nepal, 73 percent of jobs are in the informal sectors; women's participation in informal sector work is 87 percent as compared to 67 percent for men (Manandhar 2000, 9). Only 4 percent of all economically active women are engaged in the formal sectors as compared to 12 percent of men (Central Bureau of Statistics 1996).

Women's labor force participation, the nature of women's work, and their employment patterns vary according to women's socioeconomic and demographic backgrounds and their regional/geographic location. Most regions in Nepal are still rural, agrarian, and developing, and the majority of the habitants in those areas are marginal and submarginal peasant farmers. In those regions, women represent the main workforce in the household subsistence economy; they also work as agricultural laborers. Rural women also migrate internally to urban areas for work; these women work in the informal sectors in road and building construction, carpet and textile manufacturing, and in service jobs.

Women from elevated socioeconomic backgrounds and with higher levels of education tend to work in formal semiprofessional and professional occupational fields. They work as teachers, nurses, government workers, and NGO workers. Nepali women's overall participation in the formal and professional fields, especially their participation in national and international nongovernmental organizations, increased substantially after the democratic movement of the 1990s and the subsequent women's movement in Nepal.

Nepali women's international labor migration became highly visible when they gained national and international journalistic attention in relation to their labor and sexual exploitation, particularly in India and Arab nations.[14] Since the early 1990s, national and international mass media have prominently portrayed the stories of female victims of trafficking and the sex trade in Indian brothels, and the physical, emotional, and sexual abuse of female domestic workers in Arab nations.[15] The victims tend to be trafficked during the rural to urban migration process through allurements and deception. These young, unskilled women want to migrate to urban cities in hopes of better economic opportunities, but they are trafficked en route and coerced into the sex trade (Hamal Gurung 2014).

In recent years, the direction and flow of Nepali women's international migration have diversified. Today, more than in any previous decade, an increasing number of women are initiating international labor migration.[16] According to the World Bank (2011), women make up 68 percent of Nepali international labor migrants. Scholars of gender, labor, and migration issues in Nepal have persistently cited poverty and economic conditions as the main push factors for Nepali women's international labor migration (Bhadra 2007; Blaikie, Cameron, and Seddon 2001). This

14. Pioneer NGOs such as ABC/Nepal and Maiti Nepal (which work to combat human trafficking and the sex trade) publicized issues of sexual and labor exploitation when they brought victims of sex trafficking from the Indian brothels back home to Nepal.

15. The well-known documentary *The Day My God Died* (dir. Andrew Levine, Andrew Levine Productions, 2003) has raised tremendous awareness about the sex trafficking of Nepali girls and women, particularly in the Global North. It is one of the most sought-out PBS documentaries. For more information, see http://www.pbs.org/independentlens /daymygoddied/" and "http://itvs.org/films/day-my-god-died.

16. Gender discrimination in the labor migration process also contributed to the sex trafficking and labor exploitation of Nepali women. Whereas the Nepal government never imposed any bans on male international migration, it did impose a ban on female migration to the Gulf nations in 1998 (Bhadra 2009). When women continued to migrate to these countries, they encountered "a higher risk of being trafficked or becoming victims of labour exploitation" (Bhadra 2009, 85).

may have been true for most of those who traditionally migrated to India, the Gulf nations, and Southeast Asian nations to work in the domestic and service sectors. However, the experiences of women in this book (who work in the informal service and domestic sectors in Boston and New York) indicate multiple intersecting causal factors for migration to the United States. Most of these women did not move or migrate to the United States with the intention of working in the informal labor market.

In addition to changes in Nepal's political economy, Nepali women's migration and immigration to the United States should also be understood in the context of post-1990 Nepali women's movements. The 1990 People's Movement engendered women's rights movements and gender-based sociopolitical activism at the community, national, and international levels. Bhadra, a Nepali gender scholar, observes: "it was in the women's movement that 'inclusion' in its true sense was first practiced and women from all walks of life, representing Nepalese diversity (class, caste/ethnicity, culture, ecology, ability, single-hood), participated in solidarity" (2009, 81). These movements increased women's participation in the arenas of social welfare, public governance, and policy. Women's engagement in governmental and nongovernmental organizations increased their freedom of movement, as NGOs and INGOs acted as a platform for women to travel abroad to participate in international forums and workshops. The new patterns and processes of gender migration that destabilized the traditional male migration pattern emerged at this juncture of the women's movement.

Moreover, women's informal and transnational networks and connections have added dynamics to their migration process (Da 2010; Hamal Gurung 2010; Eckstein and Nguyen 2011). Few women in this book migrated from conditions of poverty at home.[17] Coming to the United States requires significant financial resources, at least a basic knowl-

---

17. When women migrate to the Gulf nations or India or Southeast Asian nations for foreign labor, they are designated as "labor migrants" in their official travel documents. The socioeconomic status of women migrating for "work" or "labor" to other nations cannot be compared to women migrating to the United States because women's initial reasons for migration are rarely listed as work or labor in the US case. Thus the established links

edge of the outside world, and transnational connections. Therefore, the majority of Nepali women who come to the United States come from relatively better socioeconomic and professional backgrounds. However, on their arrival in the United States, these women inevitably end up working in the informal service, domestic, and care work sectors.

Backgrounds of Nepali Women Workers

The information I collected on the research participants' demographic and socioeconomic backgrounds illustrates that these Nepali women migrants to the United States were quite diverse in terms of their castes/ethnicities, marital statuses, religious affiliations, and educational backgrounds.[18] The majority of the women were in their forties. Most had completed four years of college education and had earned an undergraduate degree.[19] Please see the table on participants' backgrounds in the Appendix.

The research participants' migration decisions were influenced in each case by multiple and intersecting factors. The women indicated that social, economic, political, global, and personal variables, as well as women's networks and transnational connections, influenced their decisions. As I show in the table on participants' backgrounds, less than half of the women pointed to just one factor as decisive in their migration to the United States. Only six of the thirty-five research participants identified economics as the sole reason for their migration; four identified political reasons; five identified that they migrated to visit family members or to attend a graduation ceremony of their children; three identified invitations

---

between migration and poverty for "women migrant workers" to Gulf nations is not present for women migrating to the United States.

18. In the past, the majority of labor migrants tended to be rural poor, ethnic minorities, and men.

19. Having an undergraduate degree did not mean that all the women were initially fluent in English. This is because English is not the medium of teaching in the majority of public educational institutions in Nepal. The women's command of English varied according to the undergraduate institutions that they had attended. By the time they participated in this study, however, all women had attained English-language proficiency.

from friends; three identified professional reasons, which included participation in conferences, NGO forums, and other meetings relevant to their occupation; and one identified the diversity visa lottery. The remainder indicated that a combination of personal, political, and social factors led them to migrate or immigrate to the United States.

In terms of living arrangements, the majority of the women shared an apartment with other Nepali women like themselves. Those who were employed as live-in child care providers typically resided with their employers during the weekdays and stayed with friends and family members during the weekends.

Intersecting Migration Factors

The patterns of women's migration/immigration to the United States present a complex picture. In most cases, multiple factors operated simultaneously in their migration decisions. Even participants who initially indicated a single reason had narratives that mirrored a set of intersecting factors that mediated, facilitated, and led to the decision to emigrate. The narratives below reflect such cases.

Out of thirty-five research participants, six migrated/immigrated for economic reasons, including the obligation to earn and support their families, support social organizations back home, and invest in their children's education. The economic responsibilities to support themselves and their children tended to be higher for those who were separated, widowed, or single mothers. Yet as the interviews progressed it became apparent that personal and social factors usually intersected with economic factors. Tara's story depicts this intersection of factors.

Tara was a forty-one-year-old childcare provider in New York. She came to the United States to attend a conference and ended up staying for personal, social, and economic reasons. In Nepal, Tara taught in a high school. As a community social worker, she also provided a literacy class to adult and older women. She was happily married with two children, a son and a daughter. She had a comfortable life until her husband suddenly left her and her children for another woman. She did not know his whereabouts; he did not maintain contact or send financial support. Tara became solely responsible for her children. This abrupt disruption

of conjugal life increased both her professional and domestic responsibilities. Here is how Tara recounted the incident:

> I had a nice life in Nepal. I was socially and politically very active. I
> enjoyed teaching both high school students and adult women. Every-
> thing was going very well until the day my husband left us. I still
> remember that day; my children and I had gone to my parents' house
> to celebrate a holiday. My husband didn't go with us; he decided to stay
> at home. When I returned home, I noticed that the front door was open.
> When I entered the house, I noticed that most of the stuff wasn't there,
> especially kitchen utensils, not even the stove. Initially, I thought that
> we had been robbed. Then I asked my neighbor if she had seen any-
> one breaking into my house, and she told me that my husband and his
> brother had brought a truck and taken household items. I was confused
> and shocked. I thought that maybe my husband had found a new place
> for us to move, but the reality was that he had left me alone with two
> children. I had no idea that he would do something as horrible as this.
> I had so much trust in him. This was the hardest time of my life. My
> marriage had shattered in such a bad way and I had the responsibility of
> taking care of two small children.

The financial needs and social issues that arose from her disrupted
marriage factored into Tara's decision to become a transnational working
mother. Her earnings from high school teaching were not adequate to run
the household and provide the children with suitable schooling. As the
interview progressed, Tara described additional personal and social factors that contributed to her move to the United States: "I was saddened at
how my husband had abandoned us just like that. I had never expected
that from him. I later found out that he had been having an affair with the
woman for whom he left us. It was humiliating and embarrassing. After
my husband left us, I didn't feel like staying there anymore. Oftentimes,
family, friends, and neighbors would bring up this issue; it became a topic
for gossip. And I just didn't like it."

Although financial issues were the main factor for Tara's move, personal and social issues contributed to her decision. But it was her social
networks that made migration to the United States possible. Regardless of

her decision to immigrate, without this social capital she would not have been able to make the journey. Her transnational social networks helped her gather necessary documents, obtain a visa, and find work in New York. And of course Tara herself was a well-educated professional woman with a broad worldview, which helped her to accomplish this goal.

In addition to economic factors, many migrants were influenced to move to the United States by the intersection of personal, social, and political factors related to women's shifting position in Nepali society. Gina, a forty-two-year-old childcare provider, came to Boston in 1996 with her daughter. She came from an affluent family and was educated in an elite private school in India. At the time of her move to the United States, she was teaching in a private US school in Kathmandu that mainly catered to the expatriate community. Gina came to the United States for personal, social, and political reasons. Her personal life had become political because of her relationship with her daughter's father. Because she was not formally and publicly married to the father of her child and because he was from a well-known family, the connection drew a great deal of media attention. Reporters constantly hounded her, which created unnecessary tensions and hassles for Gina. In her own words:

> In Nepal, I felt social pressure. I was unnecessarily in the limelight because of my connection with the father of my child. The media and news reporters were constantly after me and my daughter. Because of the news about my personal life, my daughter's picture was often in the newspaper. It was a kind of harassment. I just wanted to disappear from there; I just wanted to go somewhere. My cousins were living in Boston, so I called them. I informed them about my situation and told them that I wanted to come to America. They assured me that my daughter and I could stay with them; they also told me that there were childcare provider jobs available in the area.

Gina's case illustrates that she wished to leave Kathmandu because of issues related to her personal life and social situation. However, her family and kin connections in Boston made it possible for her to come to the United States. Upon her arrival, she and her daughter stayed with her cousins, who not only provided her with a place to live but also helped her find a job. As Gina said: "If it were not for my cousins, I would not have come to Boston. I felt comfortable to come because Boston was where my uncle's daughters were living. They initially did everything for me. It's important to have this kind of family support."

It is obvious that Gina's personal dilemmas and social conflicts were the immediate causes of her move. Gender norms and a culture of gender oppression seemed, however, to be the root cause of her problems. When she did not conform to the gender norms prescribed by culture and society, the media attempted to scandalize her personal life. Her only "crime" was that she chose to have a child without a formal public celebration. Her perceived rebelliousness resulted in ostracism and harassment. When the harassment began to affect her daughter's life, she decided to leave that environment. Her transnational connections and ties helped in her decision. It also helped that her family was economically sound enough to finance her trip with her daughter to the United States. Likewise, Priya, a forty-six-year-old childcare provider, came to the United States with her daughter, though in her case her daughter was an adult. Priya came simply to attend her daughter's college graduation and ultimately stayed in the United States for personal, familial, and political reasons. Her story demonstrates how her conjugal life, her daughter's presence, the political situation in Nepal, and her network of friends in Boston contributed to her staying and working in the United States. In Priya's own words: "I was planning to leave after three months. At the same time, the political situation in Nepal wasn't good. My husband had another wife. My daughter was also here and I wanted to stay longer with her. So I decided to stay longer, then I extended my visa for up to six months and after that time period I didn't go back. Then I started working. My friends told me that it's more politically and socially safe in America than in Nepal. Yes, the political situation in Nepal was not good, there was not security. My friends who are childcare providers helped me to find a nanny job."

The political situation in Nepal—especially the Maoist insurgency that fomented ongoing armed conflict and general political instability—negatively affected the safety and security of everyday life in Nepal. Some of the participants' family businesses had to be closed because the family could not regularly provide the "donations" demanded by the Maoist groups or because the frequent lengthy nationwide strikes affected the business. When the downturn in the political climate combined with economic and social elements, people gradually sought alternatives elsewhere. Two research participants indicated such factors as reasons for their migration. Their financial resources allowed them to fund their trips and their transnational ties enabled them find a place to live and work in the United States.

As indicated by the stories above, transnational networks facilitated women's ability to migrate and find a job in the United States. In some cases, these ties were fostered by the many NGOs that came to Nepal following the People's Movement. Abha, a forty-six-year-old childcare provider, came to New York in 2003 to attend a professional conference. A childhood friend was also living in New York. In Nepal, Abha was an NGO worker and her husband worked for a local municipality. Abha was a committed social worker who wanted to help her community and social organizations financially. Although she and her husband did not have to worry about basic necessities, the expenses involved with their children's education, weddings, and other social events were increasing. They had farmland, which was the main source of their food, but it did not provide an adequate flow of cash. The income from their jobs was not sufficient to meet the additional expenses. Abha borrowed cash from a relative for her airline ticket to New York. Her friend in New York was a childcare provider. When Abha shared her financial concerns, her friend suggested that she stay and work and also helped her find a job.

Women as Primary Migrants

Like Abha and Priya, other participants initially came to the United States for a short-term professional or personal reason but decided to stay as a result of the unsettled political and economic conditions in Nepal. They were told by family members to stay in the United States in order to send money back to Nepal or make a way for their children and family to join them. Hema describes how she worked toward reunifying her family.

Hema, a forty-two-year-old convenience store worker, initially came to the United States in 2002 on an invitation from an American friend. In Nepal, Hema worked as a teacher and was involved in other social organizations. Her American friend had lived and worked in Nepal for some time and they had worked together in a social organization. So when the friend provided her with all the necessary documents to visit him in New Hampshire, she came to the United States. She also had some social connections in the Boston area.

After staying with this friend for a couple of weeks, Hema went to Boston to visit her Nepali friends. There she saw them all working so hard they barely took any time off. One day, a friend who worked in a convenience store told her that the storeowner was looking for a cashier and asked her if she wanted the job. When I asked about her response, Hema said:

> I thought and thought about this work. Clearly, I was not planning to stay here long term. My husband and two sons were in Nepal. But the political situation in Nepal was getting worse day by day. Many innocent people, including social workers and teachers, were becoming the victims of political violence. The rural areas had especially become unsafe to visit, and I had to visit these areas for my work. I called home and asked my husband about this convenience store job. He told me to stay here and work. He said that I would have to do this for our sons, for their future, that I should try to work to bring them to America.

Hema had come to the United States for a personal visit, made possible through her professional and transnational affiliations. She decided to stay and work because of the political situation in Nepal. She felt a maternal and social responsibility to make a way for her sons and immediate family to come to the United States. When she decided to stay and work, she obtained her job through her network of friends. All these intersecting factors were vital in her decisions to move, work, and stay in the United States.

A small number of the participants migrated to the United States for the express purpose of immigration. Kabita, a forty-seven-year-old childcare provider, came to New York with her husband and children after her husband won the diversity visa. Kabita and her husband come from well-established families. Her husband is one of the best-known and most prominent attorneys in a western region of Nepal. When the political situation disrupted the educational system, Kabita and her husband started to worry about their children's education. The long and indefinite period of nationwide strikes called by the various political parties disrupted regular classes, delayed exams, and affected the entire school system. Given the political and social climate in the nation, Kabita's husband applied for the DV lottery to immigrate to the United States. But when they won, they had a difficult time deciding whether to immigrate. Kabita recounted:

> When we won the lottery, we were both happy and sad. It was a hard decision to make. We were socially and economically well established in Nepal. I used to work for Nepal Bank and my husband was a well-known attorney. My husband owns a law firm and he has shares in hotels. Both of us were very much engaged in social organizations and social work in our community. My husband and I wouldn't have wanted to come here if it were not for our children. We didn't want to start from scratch in America. But for our children, for their education, and for their future, we risked everything and came to America. If our political situation were stable and good in Nepal, we would not have applied for the diversity visa lottery.

Kabita indicated that coming to the United States was not her first choice, but a result of the combined political and social conditions in Nepal (which had affected her children's education) and winning the DV lottery (which gave her leverage to immigrate with the entire family without visa hassles). For the sake of their children's education and future, Kabita and her husband compromised their comfortable lifestyle to come to the United States. After a few months, however, her husband returned to Nepal. Although he periodically visits the United States, it is Kabita who resides permanently with their children. In her conjugal and work life, Kabita's experience is not different from those of other migrant women. Having legal status does not immensely affect her personal life. Her mothering has not suffered but rather intensified.

The research participants' migration trajectories reflected the complexities of women's migration decisions and processes. Personal, political, social, and cultural reasons for migration overlapped with marital status, unhappy conjugal life, single motherhood, or a desire to visit friends or attend children's graduation ceremonies. Political and economic factors, and the women's own networks and transnational connections and ties, intersected with personal and social factors. A gender-based culture of oppression (e.g., how widows, separated wives, and single mothers are perceived in Nepalese society) and unequal gender roles and relations influenced some women's decisions to migrate. As is obvious from the narratives, many participants initially came for a short time, not planning to remain in the United States. For various reasons, these women ended up working and staying longer than they had anticipated.

Conclusion

Nepali women's migration and their participation in the informal economic and service sectors is a recent trend that was stimulated by the political upheaval of the 1990s. Although personal, social, political, and economic factors all influenced their decisions to migrate, the women's transnational networks ultimately determined where they were able to settle and find jobs. Thus women's decisions to migrate involve a dynamic process of global, structural, and microeconomic changes. Their decisions were based on intersecting personal, cultural, professional, social, economic, and political factors, and their migration destinations were facilitated by the immigration policies of host nations, informal and professional networks and connections, and ethnicity and kinship.

As discussed in chapter 1, the neoclassical perspective focuses on spatial differences in supply and demand for labor (Harris and Todaro 1970; Todaro 1976). According to this perspective, a region where the supply of labor exceeds the demand will have a low wage rate, and a region where the supply does not meet the demand will have a high wage rate (Siddiqui 2001). Such wage differentials lead to labor migration from low-wage to high-wage areas. Human capital theory shares with neoclassical theory the idea that areas of origin and destination are shaped by economic inequality and spatial disparity but views migration as stemming from individual rational choices (Siddiqui 2001). In the push and pull framework, push and pull factors combine to create conditions for migration. The structural approach focuses on larger social, economic, and political inequalities and suggests that these are the specific structural conditions that compel people to migrate (Billsborrow and Zlotnik 1991).

The case of Nepali women who migrate/immigrate to the United States and work in the informal service sector is much more complex, and a single paradigm does not suffice to explain it. First, the theoretical frameworks for analyzing migration often overlap and interconnect. For example, political and economic instability and resource scarcity may push some women to move or migrate, and availability of service or informal jobs in the global cities may pull some women, but demographics, sociocultural factors, personal reasons, and social networks ultimately determine a woman's decision. The pressure of being a transnational migrant, worker, and mother is great for women like Tara who are single mothers supporting their children. But what ultimately influenced Tara's decision were social and personal factors and her transnational connections.

Similarly, Priya initially came to Boston to attend her daughter's graduation. But she decided to stay and work in Boston for multiple reasons: her conflicted conjugal relations, her connection to her daughter in the United States, and the political situation in Nepal. Her social networks played an instrumental role in getting her a job. Neither the push and pull framework nor human capital theory would be useful in analyzing her case. Gina came to the United States to escape a social and cultural climate that negatively affected her and her daughter. She came to Boston because of her familial networks and connections. Although Gina is now a single mother who works and supports her daughter, her primary reason for coming to the United States was not economic.

These women's reasons for migration intersected with factors that cannot be explained solely by globalization at the macro level. Scholars must look more deeply at how the complex combinations of demography, socioeconomic background, political economies of home nations, immigration policies of host nations, and social and transnational connections influence women's decisions and choices to migrate. If structural inequalities were a primary historical factor in shaping migration decisions of Nepalis in the past, there is now a wide range of personal, national, and global factors that shape the migration decisions of contemporary Nepalis.

3

o   o   o

The Informal Economic World

Shifting Roles, Experiences, and Identities

I learned quickly that the only way to get a good job here was to get a degree from here. That wasn't so practical for me. So the only work available for me was housecleaning, which didn't require any degree or formal training.

—Housecleaner in New York City

NEPALI WOMEN migrated to the United States for various reasons. Most of the women in this book came from better socioeconomic backgrounds and enjoyed better professional lives in Nepal than they did in the United States. In Nepal they were employed as teachers, social workers, NGO workers, and professional staff in private and governmental organizations. In the United States, most of these same women worked as childcare providers, domestics, housecleaners, restaurant workers, or cashiers in convenience stores and coffee shops. A few also worked in beauty parlors, specifically as eyebrow design specialists. Most worked in ethnically segmented labor markets where the majority of their employers were Indians and Indian Americans.[1]

Just as multiple combined factors contributed to the women's migration processes, a combination of structural and personal factors led them to informal service and care work. Structural factors included the women's US immigration status and visa categories, professional license

---

1. This employment pattern is applicable to the restaurant, beauty parlor, convenience store, childcare, and domestic work industries.

and educational credential issues, and the easy availability of informal service work. Personal factors included South Asian regional identity, demographic and cultural background, and social networks and transnational connections. The majority of the participants were drawn to jobs in informal service and care work because they did not require formal training or a license (given that their educational credentials and professional experiences from back home were not recognized by US institutions) and because their social and transnational networks provided easy access to such work (friends and relatives were the main sources of job placement). Women were also drawn to these jobs because many of them did not require legal work authorization. In some cases, women seemed to prefer work in the informal service sectors, particularly in care work for other South Asians. In other cases, they were compelled to work in these areas. Their narratives reflect how structural conditions, social and cultural capital, and personal situations influence women's decisions to enter the informal service sector.

In this chapter, I first explore some distinctive features of the informal economic sector that absorbed and attracted Nepali women. Second, I examine the women's downward career paths as they moved from Nepal to the United States. Third, I discuss the transnational networks women used to access work in the United States. Finally, I analyze the coethnic segmented labor markets in which these women were sought out by employers. I analyze how cultural similarities and transnational ties were vital to connecting potential employees and employers in ethnically cosegmented informal labor markets. I address the role of social networks, transnational connections, and South Asian cultural ties in hiring and labor practices.

I explore the following questions: What structural and cultural factors shaped women's labor conditions? How were they drawn to these jobs? Were they compelled to work in the informal sector? Did women enter this labor market by choice? If so, what made jobs in these arenas so attractive? How did the shared South Asian diaspora and identity affect relations between the women and their employers? Using both structural and intersectional frameworks, I seek to answer these questions from the women's perspectives.

The Structural Conditions of Informal Work

The "informal sector" is somewhat amorphous in its definition; activities commonly considered informal work include work that is not reported or registered, work that avoids taxes and regulation, home-based activities, social exchange activities, unofficial activities, and invisible, hidden, or shadow activities (Henry 1982; Portes and Sassen 1987). This type of work is often characterized by easy accessibility and poor work conditions. In this study, the term "informal sector work" describes non-unionized jobs obtained through word of mouth and paid in cash so that employers can avoid paying requisite taxes. These jobs were typically low-paid and required long hours.

Informal economies are embedded in larger structural conditions related to the expansion of the global capitalist economy. Economic restructuring on a worldwide scale has changed the mode, pattern, and nature of employment, creating a large demand for a casual, flexible, and informal workforce in developed countries and cities. In particular, the service, domestic, and care work sectors of the Global North have attracted and absorbed significant numbers of women, especially from the Global South.

Scholars who examine the gendered effects of globalization have also documented the feminization of international labor migration, particularly in informal service and domestic work. Paid reproductive and domestic work relies on the labor of immigrant/migrant women (Barker and Feiner 2010; Hondagneu-Sotelo 2007; Kusakabe and Pearson 2010; Piper 2004). According to Bhadra, a Nepali gender scholar, "This new characteristic of feminization of foreign labour migration is more distinct in Asia, with women constituting more than 50 per cent of the migrants" (2007, 10). Referring to Nepali women and the globalization of care work, Bhadra states: "The demand for care work in the global market has created an opportunity for Nepalese women to transform their unpaid reproductive work to paid productive work" (2007, 6).

The conditions generated by global economic restructuring were not the only factors influencing Nepali women's entrance into informal economic work. Other structural conditions and limitations arising from women's demography (race, class, gender, nationality, citizenship status, and age), US immigration policies, cultural issues, and differing educational and technical standards between host and origin nations also affected women's induction into the informal economic world. Regarding educational standards, a woman with a nursing degree in Nepal is not automatically entitled to work as a nurse in the United States. To become a qualified applicant for nursing jobs, she must go through an onerous and expensive procedure that involves applying for accreditation for her degree, taking a board exam, and applying for and obtaining a license. Other obstacles may include her legal eligibility to work in the United States and job availability. For most Nepali women professionals, considerable time and money is required to maintain their career in the United States. Lack of familiarity with the US educational system, age, and cultural factors all stand as barriers to this type of career. Most of the research participants were in their forties when they came to the United States; some indicated that to start school and go through exams and training at that age would be overwhelming. In addition, most came to the United States without the intention of staying permanently. The informal economic sector offered these women quick access to work.

Downward Sectoral Mobility from Nepal to the United States

The majority of the women in this study came from families with a relatively high socioeconomic status. Most had college-level educations and worked in the formal sectors.[2] After migrating to the United States, these women experienced a major shift in the nature of their work. Of the thirty-five research participants, twenty-nine worked in professional fields in Nepal. They held jobs in both private and public sectors such as schools, banks, hospitals, government, NGOs, and businesses. These were socially respectable jobs that allowed women to establish an occupational identity. Many of the women traveled nationally and internationally for professional development or networking.

In the United States, these women transitioned to service and domestic employment, particulary in the coethnic informal sectors. The research

---

2. Only one woman in this study lacked formal education and was not literate.

participants were predominantly employed in care work, mostly as child-care providers. The next most common category was informal service sector jobs in restaurants, convenience stores, coffee shops, and beauty salons.[3]

In addition to the availability of jobs, accessible public transportation, and social networks, undocumented workers were attracted to big cities where it was easier to become invisible to immigration or work authorities. Many of the research participants also entered the informal work sector primarily because of immigration and visa issues (albeit combined with other contributing factors). The majority of the participants were migrants who came to the United States on visa categories such as visitor and business. They came legally, but without a work permit. A very few women also came to the United States as immigrants when they or their husbands won a diversity visa lottery. Hence, although a small number of women could legally work in the United States, the majority could not. Upon obtaining an informal job in the United States, migrants with a non-immigrant visa status became undocumented workers.

Access to Informal Work through Transnational Networks

The benefits of informal sector work include easy access to jobs through networks of friends and families. These jobs do not require formal training or a license, overlook immigration or visa status, and are cash paid and tax free. These dimensions of informal economic work were appealing to some women, particularly for the middle aged. One of the New York-based restaurant and care workers stated: "Actually, these jobs really don't require legal papers. On top of that, when you have papers and if you are working legally, then you have fixed holidays and you are taxed. If you work without papers, you can have flexible hours, work many jobs, and don't have to pay tax. The same can be said about working in nail parlors."

---

3. In restaurant work, the majority worked as kitchen helpers; only a handful worked as waitresses. In the convenience store and coffee shop, they worked the cash register. See the table in the Appendix.

Mala, a fifty-one-year-old childcare worker, was also attracted to informal work because of its flexibility, lack of taxation, and cash compensation. During our interaction, she summarized the perks of her work in this way: "My work does not require any particular skills or training; I don't need to learn anything for this job. When I provide childcare, I need some skills like being caring, loving, careful, and very attentive. But I have already raised my daughter and I am experienced in this area. What I like about my work is I get paid each week; it is cash paid and without tax deduction."

The informal economy is situated within the larger structural conditions that shape transnational and coethnic social networks. Women's employment and even their choice of US city to live and work depended on these networks. The concentration of informal work in New York City and Los Angeles attracted women to these places, but social and transnational connections and ties were mediating factors. For example, Meena, a fifty-four-year-old childcare provider, initially came to Alabama to visit her son, who was a college student there. After staying with him for a couple of months, she moved to New York City to work. When asked why she did not look for a job in Alabama, Meena responded: "I had some friends and relatives living and working in New York City. I had expressed my desire to work for a few months. They told me that there are many under-the-table jobs available in New York that would not require any training or license. They assured me that if I moved to New York, they would find a job for me. I didn't know that many people in Alabama with whom I could talk about my work interests. I didn't have any connections. So, I moved to New York and within a month I started work in an Indian restaurant."

Similarly, Hema, who worked as a cashier in a convenience store in Boston, initially came to visit an American friend in New Hampshire. During a visit to Nepali friends in Boston, she received an unsolicited job offer through her friend's network. Hema's job gave her a reason to stay and work in Boston. Syama, a forty-seven-year-old childcare provider, initially came to New Hampshire and moved to Boston when she decided to stay and work in the United States. Maya, a fifty-year-old childcare provider and restaurant worker, moved from North Carolina to New York because she could not find any jobs in North Carolina but had social connections in New York City.

The research participants were also attracted to big cities like New York for their physical infrastructure and public transportation. Many of the women did not drive or have a driver's license; they mostly depended on public transportation. Hence, in addition to the concentration of informal income activities and transnational connections and ties in certain cities, access to an established and reliable public transportation system was an attractive factor. Kabita and her family chose New York City for its transportation services after they won the DV lottery. Here is how Kabita put it: "We started off in New York. Our sponsors were from California but they told us that we needed cars to get to jobs and places in California. I never drove in my life, and my son and husband could not drive here just like that. They needed a driver's license and that would have taken some time. Everything was new to us; we were not familiar with the driving rules and highways and roads."

One of the main features of informal economic sector work is that it extends employment opportunities to people with various immigration and visa statuses. Workers in the informal sector include citizens, permanent residents, refugees, asylees, undocumented immigrants and migrants, and nonimmigrants with various types of visas (students, visitors, and dependent spouses). For some workers, this sector is appealing for its access to work; others view informal work as a survival mechanism, and yet others experience informal work as a last resort when they have no other alternatives. This was the case for many of the research participants.

The participants' immigration status and visa categories intersected with their social and cultural capital to create particular work conditions and opportunities. Immigration status and visa categories factored into the women's downgraded career paths in the United States. Although these factors restricted professional job options, women had no difficulty finding jobs in the informal sector. This held true even for Maya, the only participant with no formal education. Maya had worked in New York City restaurants, private homes as a childcare provider and domestic, and beauty parlors. When asked whether she encountered any difficulties finding a job, she replied: "We never faced any difficulties finding work because there is plenty of work out there that doesn't require paperwork. In New York in low-paying jobs, paper is not an issue. . . . Wow, I must have worked in so many jobs here in New York, even if some of them were temporary jobs. All of my employers were Indians, except one Korean. I worked for a Korean-owned beauty parlor for a few months."

Maya's response illustrates how large cities like New York absorb undocumented workers into coethnic informal labor markets. However, it is a challenge for anyone to navigate such labor markets without informal networks and transnational connections.[4] Friends, family members, and acquaintances actively solicited jobs for the participants in this book. In some cases, women's contacts even recruited them to take over their own jobs before they departed for new ones.[5]

Pan-Coethnic Labor Relations

Similar to social capital, cultural capital played an important role in facilitating Nepali women's employment. Transnational connections between employers and employees and their shared cultural values, beliefs, and practices in segmented informal labor markets shaped the labor opportunities available to research participants. The cultural distinctiveness of Nepali women created a niche for them in a pan-coethnic South Asian labor market in informal service work, domestic work, and care work. The sociocultural relationships between Nepali women and their South Asian employers indicate that across the Atlantic, cultural capital were an asset for both the women and their employers.

South Asia consists of eight diverse nations with a wide variety of physical, economic, political, and cultural landscapes. Despite their great

---

4. Most of the women who worked in the service and domestic informal sectors knew one another. These women shared job information; they also discussed their wages and working and living conditions. Often they referred one another to employers. They were an important resource for new migrants in the community.

5. After establishing herself in the care work industry for some time, an experienced woman worker usually moves into a better paying job. This can be seen as a strategic plan. Five research participants replaced their own friends who were departing for a new job.

diversity, these nations share social and cultural characteristics that "bring the people of this region together as a unified whole and allow US public policy to treat this region as a bloc" (Kelkar 2011, 55). Nepali women's nationality, South Asian regional identity, ethnicity, and demographic background shaped their choices in a labor market conditioned by these social and cultural characteristics, as well as by the varied flows of South Asian migrants to the United States.

The common threads that seemed to attract South Asian employers and employees included the South Asian diaspora, regional identity, and geographical and cultural locations. One employment pattern that particularly stood out was the predominance of Indians or Indian Americans as the South Asians who most frequently employed Nepali women. This employment trend existed because Indians and Indian Americans were the highest educated professional-class South Asian immigrant community in the United States. Their immigration history in the United States was longer than that of other South Asians; they were one of the oldest and most financially and professionally established immigrant communities. Indian Americans were the highest or second highest median income earners among the ethnic minorities in the nation since their arrival in the United States in large numbers during the mid-1960s (Purkayastha and Ray 2010). In 1965, US immigration legislation "brought in a wave of educated and skilled professionals and their families. These immigrants worked white-collar jobs, earned good salaries, and were able to create and maintain a 'model minority' image" (Kelkar 2011, 57). This relatively privileged socioeconomic status compared with other South Asian immigrant communities put Indians and Indian Americans in a position to employ other South Asian immigrants. Faced with a large informal labor pool, Indian Americans chose care workers whose culture closely approximated their own.

Within the South Asian informal labor markets, Nepali women preferred to work for Indian employers.[6] One obvious explanation for this

6. Since Nepalis are a new and emerging immigrant community, the number of Nepali professionals in the United States is quite small. Although the chance of Nepalis becoming

pattern is the ongoing sociocultural and political-economic relationship between India and Nepal as neighboring nations. Regarding the political economy, the relationship between these countries is best understood through Wallerstein's core (center) and dependency (peripheral) framework.[7] As a landlocked country, Nepal is dependent on India for its major exports and imports. Historically, Indian cities have also provided a source of employment for poor Nepali workers (as discussed in chapter 2). The employer-employee relation between Indians and Nepalis dates back to the fourteenth century. With the exception of Gurkha soldiers, Nepali labor migrants in India have primarily remained in unskilled, lower paying, low-status job sectors such as construction, tea plantations, domestic work, and restaurants.

Regarding sociocultural relationships between the two nations, India and Nepal have the largest Hindu populations of all nations and share major Hindu festivals such as Durga Puja and Deepavali. Indians and Nepalis alike make pilgrimages to Hindu and Buddhist religious sites in both countries. The Devanagari script is shared across the Nepali language and the Hindi language. Similarities also exist in lifestyle, entertainment, food habits, and dress across India and Nepal.

These similarities factored into Indian employers' preference to hire Nepali women and Nepali women's preference to work for Indian employers. This was particularly prominent for live-in childcare providers and domestics. Women employed as childcare providers in Indian families were sought for their mothering roles and shared culture, food, and language. In some cases, the Indian family specifically employed Nepali women in the hope that their children would learn the Hindi language and become acquainted with Indian and Nepali food.

Some Nepali live-in childcare providers preferred to work in Indian households for these same reasons. New immigrants/migrants in the

---

employers is relatively slim compared with their Indian counterparts, the trend has already begun. One research participant was a childcare provider for a Nepali professional couple. It will be interesting to see whether Nepalis will prefer to work for other Nepalis when there are more Nepali professionals and entrepreneurs in the United States.

7. See Wallerstein (2004) for an in-depth world-system analysis.

initial stages of their work felt safe and comfortable as live-in domestics for Indian families. This was also true of older women (in their late forties and fifties), those who did not have professional backgrounds back home, and those without command of the English language. For some, religion also seemed to be a major factor in their preference in working for an Indian Hindu family. Such was the case for Abha. What mattered most to Abha was the cultural and religious background she shared with her Indian Hindu employer. She stated: "When I was in Nepal, I had wished to make a temple for Goddess Durga. I didn't have enough money so I borrowed about 1 lakh from the NGO that I worked in and hired constructors to build a temple. I will also place a statue of Goddess Durga in the temple. I'm a true devotee of the goddess. My employers are also devotees of Goddess Durga. When I heard that, I felt like it was God's decision to bring me to their house."

Entertainment, one of the main aspects of culture, mirrors the arts, religions, customs, lifestyles, and social, political, and economic landscapes and issues of a society. Indian songs, Bollywood films and TV series, and religious legends and plays have heavily influenced the Nepali community. The women in this book were no exception to this cultural and media consumerism; many indicated their continuing interest in Bollywood films and TV. For some, the ability to consume this form of entertainment was a perk of working in an Indian household. During her job interview, Abha was thrilled to see videocassettes of the Mahabharata and Ramayana religious narratives. While working, she rarely had time to watch such videos, but she was happy to know that these cultural tokens were there. They were a reminder of home: "When I was in Nepal, I used to watch both the Mahabharata and Ramayana on TV. I am familiar with the stories and all the teachings. So when I saw those videocassettes in the house, I got very excited. When I watch these episodes, I forget that I am in America. I feel like I am at home in Nepal."

Far away from her home, family, and community, the Mahabharata and Ramayana TV shows provided Abha continuity with her home life in Nepal. They gave her a sense of security, comfort, and belonging and made her adjustment to a foreign land, culture, and environment easier. The Nepali diaspora thus emerged in and comerged with the pan-coethnic

Indian employer/family. The affluence of pan-coethnic South Asians, the South Asian diaspora, geopolitical history, and sociocultural ties between Nepal and India bring Indian employers and Nepali workers together in American informal labor markets.

Conclusion

Most of the women in this book came from professional occupational backgrounds and experienced downward occupational mobility in the United States. Their cases illustrate that they were drawn to the informal, service, and coethnic labor markets by both personal and structural factors. Women were both attracted and compelled to work in such labor markets, which offered perks and survival mechanisms. For some women, the tax-free cash income and easy entry and exit were appealing personal factors. Lack of legal immigrant status was one of the prominent structural factors that compelled women's entrance into these markets. Whether the reasons were personal or structural, women relied a great deal on their social networks and transnational connections to seek and obtain jobs in informal service and coethnic labor markets.

The social and cultural aspects of the informal economy were quite visible in the lives of both employees and employers, which led to easily accessible, invisible domestic service, social exchange, and social network-based employment as discussed by Gaughan and Ferman (1987). The majority of the participants obtained their jobs by word of mouth; their social and transnational networks provided the crucial links to accessing work. Friends, family members, and acquaintances already in care work played an influential role in connecting Nepali women migrants with jobs. Social and transnational ties helped women acquire jobs and find places to live after they arrived in the United States. The narratives in the previous chapter and section have already illustrated such patterns, and the narratives in chapter 6 further illustrate the centrality of women's agency and the power of their social and transnational connections.

4

o   o   o

Informal Economic Work

Delusions, Challenges, and Contradictions

> I was hired to work five days a week. . . . But often I work during the
> weekend. . . . My working day starts at 7 a.m. and usually ends after din-
> ner around 9 p.m. . . . And sometimes it is even longer, especially when
> my employers are attending a social event . . . or when there is a party
> at home.
>
> —Childcare provider in New York City

IN THE PREVIOUS CHAPTER, I examined the factors that absorb and
attract Nepali to the informal pan-coethnic labor market. In this chapter, I focus on women's labor experiences in service and domestic work.
Using an intersectional framework, I analyze labor, labor relations, and
work conditions in relation to women's race, class, gender, nationality, and
immigration status. I begin by discussing the intersectional framework as
a theory and a method to contextualize women's work experiences. The
chapter centers on women's work lives to illustrate their vulnerability in
the workplace. The chapter also demonstrates the contradictory and paradoxical relationships that form between Nepali women and their South
Asian Indian employers in the ethnically segmented labor markets.

Crossroads of Gendered Labor: Race, Class, Gender, Nationality, and Citizenship Status

When the women in this book moved to the United States and began
to work in the informal service and domestic sectors, they became more
than transnational workers. The geographic shift also brought a shift in

their racial and ethnic identities, gender positions, social class, and occupations. These shifts created new identities, roles and statuses, images,
perceptions, and categories of experience. In US society, Nepali women
from all caste and ethnic groups became "women of color." In terms of
work position and status, they became low-paid workers in the lowest
tier of service and domestic informal economic sectors, with jobs such as
childcare provider, housecleaner, restaurant worker, and other informal
worker roles. In these positions, women encountered labor exploitation
and emotional abuse. Exploitative labor practices included accusations of
stealing, threats with regard to their immigration status, and degrading
racist and classist terminology. The women's voices illustrate that becoming a service, domestic, or care worker in the informal sector was a racialized and gendered process.

Women's spatial and occupational shifts vis-à-vis their gender, race,
and class positions in the informal and service economic sectors lead to
exploitation, oppression, and subordination (Chang 2000; Glenn 1986;
Rollins 1985; Romero 1992, 2005). "Domestic work is deeply imbedded in
hierarchies of class, gender, race, ethnicity, and nationality" (Brown and
Misra 2003, 502). Labor exploitation occurs at the intersection of race, ethnicity, class, gender, sexuality, nationality, and legal citizenship status,
and its effects are often experienced simultaneously across these categories of personal identity, not separately (Collins 1990; Glenn 2002; Zinn
and Dill 1993).

From colonial times to the present global era, women in general and
women of color and immigrant/migrant women in particular have disproportionately shouldered the burden of domestic and reproductive
labor in the United States (Glenn 1986; Rollins 1985; Romero 1992). The
nature and pattern of Nepali women's work confirms this (see chapter 3).
A disproportionate number of Nepali women work in service and care
work sectors despite their educational and professional backgrounds in
Nepal. Studies consistently report that among migrant and immigrant
women workers, women of color and those without legal permission to
work (and thus no political and legal rights) are subject to the most dehumanizing abuse and exploitation (Chang 2000; Rollins 1985; Hondagneu-
Sotelo 1997, 2007).

Placing women's narratives in the center and focusing on their lived experiences, this chapter describes the typical labor conditions and practices experienced by these workers. It demonstrates that intersecting statuses of race, class, gender, nationality, and immigration status all influence their work experiences. It also describes how women's labor experiences differ between domestic/care work and service work. Finally, the chapter addresses how the South Asian diaspora and identity affect labor relations between the women and their South Asian employers as they are integrated into a distinctly pan-coethnic labor market.

Work Conditions and Labor Relations: Long Days, Long Nights

Because the employment and hiring process in the informal labor market typically involves both employers' and workers' social networks, almost all the participants in this study obtained employment through friends, families, and fellow immigrant/migrant communities. Their employment process did not include legal contracts or formal procedures; all terms of employment, including wages and hours, were discussed verbally. The employment and hiring pattern relied totally on a complex web of social and informal networks that not only helped women find employment but also provided potential employers with specific information on the women's backgrounds.

In general, employers had complete autonomy in hiring and deciding the wage, work hours, and all other work-related policies.[1] They could change these rules at any time without consulting the workers. These jobs were unregulated; workers had no benefits and were left unprotected from labor violations. Women's only job benefits were the room and board included for live-in nannies.

Almost all of the women encountered some form of labor exploitation or emotional abuse. The degree of exploitation varied across workplaces, however. Exploitative practices included work without pay, longer

---

1. In some cases—for example, if women were being recruited to replace a family member or a friend's position—their relatives/friends could have some say in determining the wage.

work hours than agreed on, and work during the weekend.[2] The majority of the women, especially those who were hired as childcare providers, ended up doing additional domestic work. Although the additional work increased their work hours, their pay remained the same. Shanti, a forty-eight-year-old Nepali woman, was hired to look after two small children for a professional Catholic family in a suburb of Boston. In addition, she also performed all the domestic work without any additional compensation. After five years of work, her weekly pay increased from $250 to $350. Such work experiences were not atypical. Shanti's work experiences in two different families provide insight into her work conditions: "I had to look after two small children. I had to do other tasks besides babysitting, like housekeeping. They made me clean the house and do the laundry but didn't make me cook food, unlike Indian employers. Since I was a live-in babysitter, I sometimes even had to work until 11 p.m. I started to work at $250 per week. Now that I think of it, it was brutal. I worked from 8 a.m. until around 7 p.m. in the evening, long hours. And I worked there for seven years. Later on, they raised it to $350."

Shanti's reference to the Indian families draws on a perception among Nepali workers about the exploitative conditions that existed in the pan-coethnic labor market. However, even with non-South Asian families, Shanti experienced considerable exploitation. Her experiences with another upper-class family in the Newton area illustrate the magnitude of her labor exploitation as well as emotional abuse and humiliation: "I worked for another rich American family.[3] It was very odd, now that I think about it. The first six weeks I worked for them, they said that I wouldn't get paid because it was my training period. The wife had a bad temper. She would get angry with me easily. Once I did not place the

---

2. During an initial employment interview, women were told they would get weekends off. However, after they were hired, many were asked and expected to work during weekends. The fact that women were expected to work whenever they were asked to reflects their lack of control over their labor.

3. Like other participants, Shanti used the term "American family" to refer specifically to *white* American families.

food exactly the way she would, and when she opened the freezer, she got very angry. She started to throw things on the floor and she used the "F" word toward me. I felt so bad and humiliated, and I quit that job." Shanti's experiences in both households exemplified workers' vulnerability. The employers wielded enormous power over the workers, and—at least in these two cases—they abused that power.

How does this differ from the Indian employers that Shanti referred to in her narrative earlier? Tara's experiences provide some insight into the work conditions in pan-coethnic households. Tara worked as a live-in nanny in Flushing, New York. Her Indian employers hired her knowing that she did not have a work permit. She was hired to work Monday through Friday, from 8 a.m. to 6 p.m. The arrangement was that at the end of her workday on Friday, she would leave her employer's home and stay with her friends. She would then come back to work on Sunday night. In reality, the arrangement operated very differently. On weekdays, she always worked longer than the set hours. She normally started work before 7 a.m. and continued until 7 p.m., after the family's dinner. Sometimes, even during the night, if the employers' child could not go to sleep, the mother brought him to Tara, and Tara would be back on the job trying to make the child go to sleep. Here is how Tara recounted it: "I earned $250 per week, I also did household chores. . . . The child was very close to me. He would even sleep in my room. The child would cry in the middle of the night and the mother would bring the child into my room and leave him there."

This quote illustrates Tara's emotional closeness with the child and the trust the biological mother had in Tara. It also reflects Tara's gratification and contentment regarding her relationship with the child. But intimacy and trust did not equalize the hierarchical labor relationship between Tara and her employers. Tara had no control over her labor and labor conditions. As a live-in nanny, she was also expected to provide other domestic services. When Tara started to cook Nepali food for herself, her employer asked her to increase the amount so they could also eat the same food (the similarities between Nepali and some Indian cuisines seemed to factor into this particular issue). Cooking thus became another daily chore. She was asked to clean the house and do the laundry. These household tasks were not discussed during hiring and were not part of her job description, but she had to perform them. Clearly, as a newcomer without a work permit in New York, Tara could not say no to her employers' demands. The expectation that she do the laundry started with the baby's clothes but gradually expanded to include adult clothing. Tara's workload increased significantly but her wage remained the same.

Tara eventually quit her job. When asked what triggered her decision to leave, Tara replied: "I worked for this family for more than a year. My workload kept increasing, but my wage remained the same. I had to cook, clean, I was constantly working even at night. . . . I asked them to raise my wage and they told me to wait for another year. So I quit."

Tara accepted another live-in nanny position. She worked for a Jewish family taking care of their three children. Her work schedule and arrangements were similar to her previous job, but because she was taking care of three children, her wage was double that of her previous job. In this position, Tara did not have to cook or clean, but her work hours were longer—from 7 a.m. to 7 p.m. Even after her work hours, the children often came to her room and engaged her in various activities.

Although the work arrangement was such that Tara could leave Friday night and return Sunday night, any social event at her employers' house or social engagement outside their house would restrict her free time during the weekend. On such occasions, she had to look after the children and could not leave the house. Working these extra hours did not increase her salary, and none of these work policies were discussed during the hiring process.

Tara tolerated these conditions because of her immigration status. Although her employers were vague about her weekend obligations during the hiring process, they also did not ask whether she was eligible to work or check any of her documents. As with her previous employer, Tara was hired by employers who tacitly understood that she did not have work documents: "I came here on a visitor visa. I don't have a work permit. I have seen that a lot of women who don't have a work permit work in either nail salons or in housekeeping. It is very difficult to be under the control of another person because sometimes I have to work on the weekends when I want to go out to Nepali gatherings."

Tara was connected to these employers through her circle of friends who were doing similar work. During the hiring interview, her employers asked how long she had been in the United States and whether she had ever had a childcare job. Once they knew she had been in the country for about eighteen months and had already been employed in childcare, they asked her to come to work the following Monday (she was interviewed on a Saturday). Tara's employers knew about her socioeconomic and cultural background and immigration status through the friend who introduced them.

Tara's background and immigration status made her an ideal worker. In her first week on the job, Tara found out that her employers were looking for someone who would stay in the job for a long time. She also learned that taking care of these children would be challenging. On her second day at work, a neighbor warned her about the children's wild and violent behaviors. Tara recounted: "The neighbor told me that they've already had twelve nannies. I was kind of nervous. Later, I understood why there were twelve nannies. The children really were very wild. They would throw anything and everything at each other. They would fight with each other and they even hit me so many times. One of my best friends had to look after them for a day because I was sick, and she told me that she couldn't deal with those kids."

During the job interview, Tara's employers did not mention the children's personalities and behavior. Tara bore their violent outbursts with a great deal of patience and tolerance, but over time their behavior began to wear on her emotional well-being. Once, when she was ill and trying to rest, the children came into Tara's room and started to jump on her bed. They shouted and threw things at each other. What bothered Tara the most was that the parents did not say or do anything to stop the children, nor did they apologize for the children's behavior. According to Tara, their attitude was that because Tara was hired to take care of the children, she should be expected to put up with their extreme bad behavior. Tara suffered silently; her problems were invisible.

Meena's reason for quitting her job provides another perspective. Meena was employed by an Indian family to provide childcare. She was automatically expected to combine this work with other domestic chores such as cooking and cleaning. Her workload increased without any commensurate increase in pay. Meena enjoyed cooking, so she enthusiastically combined her care work with cooking. But she decided to quit the job when her employers demanded a totally different kind of extra work that took a long time to complete and had to be done in excessive heat. In Meena's own words: "I was hired to babysit the kid. I decided to quit because they asked me to do more than they had hired me for. . . . Something happened that made me want to quit. Last June, they brought forty to fifty flower pots and they asked me to water them every day and it was so hot outside. Toward the end of June, I told them that I couldn't do that job anymore. I told them that I was hired to care for their son, not to water their flowers, so I ended up quitting."

Both the gradual increase in workload and the demand for a totally different kind of work contributed to Meena's decision to quit her job. Initially she was not hired to cook, but when cooking was added to her tasks, she did not mind; she was used to doing it for her family back home. But she could not bear to spend a large part of her day watering plants in hot weather. Meena perceived this demand as insulting. When she was cooking and cleaning, she thought of herself as a family member, but when she was asked to water plants she felt like a servant.

Other factors might have indirectly contributed to Meena's decision to quit her job. It could be that she was not used to doing gardening work, as many middle- and upper-middle-class Nepalis employ gardeners to take care of their yards. For that reason, she may have considered domestic work outside the home demeaning and inferior, and felt humiliated by it. Perhaps the line between considering herself a family member or a servant became very clear when the employer demanded that she water plants.

Seema, a forty-one-year-old nanny, worked for an Indian family in New York. She did not have work documents and her employers did not inquire about her immigration status, which was implicit in the employment relation as an unspoken truth. Her employers made all the decisions regarding labor employment at the time of hiring, including the days, hours, and workload. In practice, however, the employers did not adhere to the conditions they themselves had set. For example, Seema was initially told that she would work during the week only, but she was actually expected to work many weekends. She was also asked to make up for days when the family vacationed away from home. These labor relations produced economic and emotional suffering for Seema:

> When I took care of the child, I thought of him as my own kid. It really hurt me when the baby cried, and I wanted to take care of him. But the employers think of childcare as a business because they can say I pay you for this and I pay you for that. This kind of attitude really hurts my feelings. One time they had gone for a vacation and she asked me if I could work and make up one Saturday. I really didn't like that. Finally, I had the courage to tell her that I couldn't convince my heart about what she had said. I was always ready to work and I considered them like my family, and why should I work for a makeup when they had gone for a vacation?

In a follow-up interview with Seema during summer 2009, I learned that she was not paid when the family was away on vacation. Despite explicit rules laid out during the hiring process, over the course of time the family felt entitled to ask Seema to "make up" a day of labor that she was never compensated for in the first place.

Alongside exploitative labor conditions, domestic workers face emotional abuse. Two research participants faced such abuse when they were accused of stealing. Kabita was one of these two wrongly accused women. She had worked in various places in New York as a childcare provider, domestic, and restaurant worker. All her employers were South Asians and the majority were Indians. Like many other women, when Kabita started working as a childcare provider, she discovered that her work also entailed an expanding list of household chores. But what really made the work conditions unbearable for Kabita was that she was accused of stealing, which intensified her emotional suffering:

> I worked for a professional Indian family in Brooklyn, New York. I was hired as a live-out nanny to provide childcare for their children; they had two sons. But I did all sorts of domestic work there, from laundry to making food. I never worked so hard in my whole life. I regretted

coming here. They liked my cooking, and I didn't mind that. I even made snacks for the kids. But the wife had a habit of accusing me of things that I did not do. One day, she accused me of stealing a silver cup, which was used for the baby's feeding. I told her I didn't take it but she didn't trust me. Every day, she would inquire about it. I cried a lot . . . I had never cried so much like that in my life. I wanted to quit right then, but I wanted to wait until the cup was found. I knew it was inside the house somewhere. I prayed to Lord Ganesh every day. One day, when I came to work, she told me that they had found the cup. She told me that it was buried under the huge piles of toys. When I heard this, my tears started to roll but with happiness. I felt relieved, free of the stealing accusation. The next morning, I bought ladoos [a special Nepali sweet] and went to the Hindu temple and offered them to Ganesh. Then I went to work, and that day I gave her notice and in two weeks I left the place. That stealing accusation still haunts me. This is my most unforgettable memory working in America.

Maya, another New York-based migrant, also worked in various informal sectors as a childcare provider, restaurant worker, convenience store clerk, and assistant in a beauty salon. Her work experiences were similar to those of other women employed in the same sectors. One day while she was working at a Pakistani-owned convenience store, the register had a cash shortage of $60. Although she did not work as a cashier, her employer implied she had taken the cash and fired her. Maya's declaration of innocence did not matter. The worst part was that Maya was never paid for her final work period. As an undocumented worker without legal rights she had little recourse but to leave her job quietly but with a feeling of injustice.

The informal labor market provided Shanti, Kabita, Maya, Meena, and Seema with easy access to jobs in service and care work. It is also true that some women preferred to work for Indian families for sociocultural reasons. Irrespective of whether they worked for Indians or non-Indians, these women were vulnerable to emotional abuse, injustice, and feelings of helplessness. Structural factors including immigration status, visa categories, gender, nationality, and citizenship conditioned their work choices, work conditions, and labor relations. As previous studies have reported, female migrants without proper work documents have limited control over their work conditions (Romero 1992; Rollins 1985). The women were afraid to negotiate with employers about work policies because of their fear of deportation. There was no open communication between women and their employers where the workers could address unfair work conditions and practices. When work conditions became unbearable, women just quit their jobs.

Moving from one job to another was a typical pattern in these women's work lives. By the time of our interviews, most of the women had already changed jobs two or three times. The average duration of women's first jobs varied from three months to two years. Exploitative work conditions and the oppressive labor relations contributed to women's decisions to leave, but mediating factors also had an influence. These factors included access to other job options, work experience, and immigration status. For example, more experienced workers felt more capable of finding another job if they left their employer owing to their networks and work history. Their nationality—South Asian origin and broad cultural similarities with some North Indians—opened up some jobs for them. Immigration status was the most important factor mediating women's ability to leave, however. Women with legal work authorization had the most freedom to select a better job.

Racialized Gendered Citizens: Prejudice and Discrimination

Feminists who are women of color have "analyzed domestic work as a reflection of national race relations . . . [and] argued that the personal subordination embedded in employee-employer relationships was grounded in race relations" (Romero 2007, 268). In addition to labor exploitation and emotional abuse, Nepali women workers encounter racism, classism, humiliation, and prejudice because of their nationality and immigration status. Nepal's position in the global political economy—in particular, Nepal's national economic condition and its image as one of the poorest nations of the world—seemed to inform employers' attitudes toward women workers. Most of the women in this book came from relatively better socioeconomic positions. However, because of their national identity, race, and class positions in the labor market, they were lumped into a single category: poor Nepali women from one of the poorest nations who were migrating/immigrating to the United States in their desperation to earn dollars.

Interestingly, degrading stereotypes based on nationality were more common among the pan-coethnic employers. Indian employers appreciated Nepali workers for their cultural similarities, but some also looked down on these workers for their Nepali national identity. For example, Binta, a forty-two-year-old childcare provider based in New York City who had previously worked for different Indian families, recalled her employer's prejudiced attitudes at her first job: "People think of Nepalese as very poor. Like, when I went to work in my first job, the employer showed me the microwave, washing machine, and dishwasher like I had never seen such things before. I humbly told her that I had all of that in my house in Nepal because I could afford it. I really don't like the way they try to demean us. . . . The fact that racism exists is very sad."

Binta's experience reflects the classist attitude of her employer and others who saw Nepalis as necessarily economically inferior. Although in the United States Indians and Nepalis are lumped into a single pan-ethnic category as South Asian, outside of this context Indians and Nepalis do not see themselves as part of the same group. Nationality, religion, and caste are all salient categories that people from this region use to locate their own status in relation to others. In the United States, race is most often assessed through the association of immediately observed phenotypes with particular groups; in this context, Nepalis (and Indians) are often classified and treated as South Asian but also as East Asian, Middle Eastern, black, or Hispanic (Purkayastha 2005). A very different social understanding of race exists in India and Nepal.[4] Within a racial category,

4. In Nepal, caste- and ethnic-based classifications are more salient than race-based classifications, unlike in the United States where race is the main axis of social hierarchies. Governmental and nongovernmental offices, including the Census Bureau of Nepal, use caste and ethnicity to classify people into different groups. Broadly speaking there are two main races in Nepal: Indo-Aryan and Mongoloid. The term "Mongol" also refers to the "Tibeto-Burman"-speaking ethnic community in Nepal. After the democratic movement

there are various castes and subcastes and ethnic categories and groups. The historical caste-based ranking and classification of people in India and Nepal had created social, political, and economic hierarchies along race, caste, and ethnic lines. It is not clear, however, to what extent the hierarchical caste- and ethnic-based classifications of Indians and Nepalis transferred and manifested across the Atlantic. It is also not clear to what degree the coethnic employers' and employees' races, castes, and ethnicities interacted and resulted in exploitative and abusive labor conditions.

According to US understandings of race as phenotype, racism would not seem to be a factor in relations among Indian employers and Nepali workers. However, these relations were marked by a racialized prejudice based on stereotypes of nation and nationality. A few of the women's narratives suggest strong interactions among gender, social class, nationality, and citizenship in generating particular attitudes and stereotypes on the part of employers.

Syama worked for a professional Indian family in a Boston suburb. Like Binta, she encountered humiliating treatment from her employers. During her second day on the job, Syama's employer revealed her condescending attitude toward Nepali women: "I was feeding the child and the mother came and started to talk with me. She told me I would be rich pretty soon, then she asked me, "Do you know how much a dollar is?" Then she told me it's almost 80 Nepali rupees. Then she said, "You haven't seen a dollar in Nepal, have you? You came to the United States to earn dollars, right? So you have to work hard to earn this much money: you have to please us, you have to follow our instructions, and you have to obey us. Otherwise you won't earn dollars and will remain poor forever."

This quote reflects the prejudiced views of her employer toward Nepal and Nepalis, particularly in relation to their economic condition. The employer's attitude was that Nepal is a poor country and all Nepalis are

---

of 1990s, the term "Mongol" has also become a contested and political issue. See Hangen's article "Race and the Politics of Identity in Nepal" (2005) for an in-depth discussion on this particular issue. See also Bista (1987, 1991); Gurung (1998); Pradhan (2000); and Lal (2000) for more information about the compositions and dynamics of race, caste, and ethnicity in Nepal.

poor. The quote also indicates the colonial mentality of Indian employers who considered Nepali women to be servants. Syama's employer expected her to serve and obey.

Not surprisingly, Syama's work conditions were similar to the exploitative conditions experienced by many other participants. Whenever her employer hosted house parties or the child became sick, Syama was expected to forego her time off. Moreover, because she did not drive, Syama had to rely on her employers to provide transportation to the commuter train station Friday evening and from the station Sunday evening. Many weekends, she remained in her employers' home.

Another New York-based childcare provider who encountered a similar classist and prejudiced attitude on the part of her employer quit her job within a month. As she recounted: "When I went to this family to work, they were very prejudiced about Nepal. They thought that all Nepalese were poor and couldn't afford food or clothing and were only suitable as servants. They showed this attitude toward me as well, and it was very difficult for me. I stayed there for three weeks and after that I lost my patience with them so I left that place."

Syama's and this worker's voices indicate that Indian employers' stereotypes of Nepal and Nepalis factored into their disdain for the women workers. In deciphering these prejudiced behaviors and attitudes within "coethnic" labor markets, we need to pay particular attention to Nepal's status in South Asian regional geopolitics and its political economic relationships with its South Asian neighbors. In the case of Indian employers and Nepali women workers, we need to understand Indo-Nepali relationships in a historical context. Nepal is often viewed as the periphery of India. As I discussed in chapter 2, Nepal still depends on India for its major economic activities, such as import and export trade, commerce and business, and labor migration and remittances. Nepal's past and current economic dependency on India, including its history of labor migration, may have influenced Indian employers' perceptions of Nepali women workers' class position.

This complicates the definition of pan-coethnic labor markets established in the previous chapter. Whereas much of the US migration literature groups Nepalis and Indians together under the category of "South

Asian," nuances and hierarchies exist within this broad category. Consistent with nationality-based discrimination identified by Parillo (2008), these workers experienced interethnic prejudice *within* a pan-coethnic labor market.

An analysis from multiple jeopardy perspectives reveals that these combined and compounding factors left women with multiple disadvantages (King 1989). Thus, nationality-based discrimination negatively affected workers who were already in exploitative and abusive labor conditions because of their gender, social class position, immigration status, nationality, and citizenship.

Studies have consistently shown that domestic and care workers, both women of color and immigrant/migrant women, are at the very bottom of the job hierarchy and have no control over their labor and labor conditions (Chang 2000; Glenn 1986; Rollins 1985; Romero 1992; Hondagneu-Sotelo 2007). The Nepali women also followed this pattern; they worked in the lowest tier of the informal service and domestic sectors. Their experiences mirrored the lives of many female domestic workers reported in the Rollins (1985) study. In both studies, women experienced feelings of servitude, social isolation, dependency, marginalization, and humiliation. These studies also reflect women's desire to be treated as human beings. They quit their jobs not only because the work conditions became unreasonable but also because their human dignity had been violated and the psychological exploitation had become unbearable.

Between Private and Public Sphere Service and Care Work: Roles and Experiences

At the time of the interviews, the majority of the women indicated childcare as their primary job. However, their work histories were divided into three distinctive patterns: (1) Mobile workers switched jobs among childcare, restaurant work, and work in other informal service jobs such as beauty parlors. (2) Dual workers conducted care work alongside other jobs in the informal service sector. (3) Combined workers were in jobs with no clear boundaries between care work and domestic work (e.g., women hired as childcare providers also performed domestic work such as housecleaning and cooking). So how do women's work experiences, work conditions, and labor relations differ in noncare work? Are there significant differences between domestic care work and nondomestic care work? Do women prefer care work to noncare work?

Kabita was a mobile worker in New York City. Throughout her time in the United States, Kabita had changed jobs for various reasons. She left care work when she was accused of stealing a silver cup. She also worked in restaurants where she had positive and negative experiences. Kabita's case illustrates the mobility of women between service work, which is performed publicly, and domestic work, which is performed in more private settings. Kabita contrasted her experiences as a domestic worker to a worker in a restaurant in the following manner: "After I left care work, I began work as a cashier at an Indian restaurant. The job and the pay were good, and I got free food there. I also got tips. The owner was a really good and educated person. He didn't let me do other tasks; he insisted that I work just as the cashier. I worked there for two years, and then I went to Nepal for a few months. When I got back to the States, I worked at another Indian restaurant as a cashier. But they made me do everything. I had to clean, pick up the dishes, mop the floor, clean the bathroom. I just could not do it, so I quit." In the second restaurant, Kabita experienced expanding labor expectations, similar to her experience in domestic service.

Kabita's experience of straightforward labor conditions in the first restaurant was exceptional among the participants. Two other restaurant workers shared experiences similar to Kabita's in the second restaurant. Both Rani and Lata were in their late thirties. Rani worked in a coffee shop and Lata worked in a restaurant in Boston. When I asked Rani about her work experience, she recounted, "We are busy here all the time. I mop the floor, I make coffee, and I bake. I get a lunch break for half an hour, that's all. By the end of the day, I am so tired." Lata's restaurant work was even more physically demanding: "Supposedly, I am a waitress. But I do everything—clean tables, dishes, receive phone and take-out orders. And if I am working the night shift, I vacuum and clean the restaurant. And sometimes I clean the dishes." Although some of these tasks may be expected in a coffee shop or small family-run business, Rani and Lata's work experiences indicate that the workloads and work conditions in noncare informal sectors are similar to those in the domestic sectors.

According to human capital theory, international migrants are supposed to move from one place to another for better job opportunities, socioeconomic mobility, and better lives. This is not necessarily the case with Nepali women who have moved to America. These women work in degrading informal income-generating sectors at a level well below that of their educational and skill levels back home. For example, Syama was a nurse and a social worker in Nepal. Prior to her childcare work in the United States, she worked in an Indian restaurant in Boston. She recalled her first job: "Picking and cleaning the dirty dishes and mopping the floor was not a good experience at all. Many times I went to the restroom and backdoors of the kitchen and cried. When my coworkers saw me crying, I would tell them that it was because I missed my home. . . . I had a respectable job in Nepal, many people knew me through my work. This job did not have any status."

These particular groups of women were not used to working in such demeaning conditions. They were not used to cleaning tables and mopping floors. As housewives they might have done something similar in their households, but they were not accustomed to doing such tasks in public arenas. Sarina, a forty-year-old restaurant worker and childcare provider, was an NGO worker in Nepal. Upon her arrival in Boston, she worked two jobs. Both employers were Indians. On the weekends, Sarina worked at a restaurant manning the cash register, taking food orders, cleaning tables, and washing dishes. On weekdays, she worked as a full-time nanny for a toddler. Sarina had a college education, and through her NGO work in Nepal she had visited other countries as a professional. The work life of a restaurant worker and childcare provider and the labor relations in service and care work were new to her. She recounted her downward occupational shift in the United States: "I have become a wageworker here; there is no possibility for upper mobility. I worked in an NGO in Nepal and my job was respectable. I used to travel a lot. My education and skills are useless here. It would be nice to have a good job, but I don't have a work permit. So I am stuck in such jobs."

When asked about her job experience in care work and noncare work, and whether one work setting was better than the other, Sarina replied, "Babysitting is socially alienating and monotonous, and restaurant work physically exhausting. It is difficult to say which work or work setting is better than the other."

Sony was a twenty-eight-year-old part-time live-out nanny and a cashier at a laundromat in Boston. She was a teacher and had been working toward an MBA degree at Kathmandu University in Nepal. Referring to her current job in the United States, she said, "This is my first time working as a nanny and as a helper in a laundry place. In Nepal, I taught school, worked in an NGO, and helped my husband's business. This is definitely not an uplifting job." When asked about the difference between her nanny and laundromat jobs, she replied: "The nanny job is insular; I feel socially isolated just being inside the house and taking care of the baby. I don't get to interact with the outside world. Although I don't have to use my brain too much, taking care of a baby is a stressful and responsible job. In my other job, I get to talk and meet with all kinds of people. Some regular customers have become my friends. My time goes fast, and I don't feel stress. Although this job has nothing to do with my previous work experience or educational background, I am enjoying meeting and interacting with people and making friends."

Women workers experienced the physical and emotional demands of service work, and they were aware that such jobs are not suitable in the long run. Rita, a thirty-eight-year-old New York-based housecleaner, liked the different aspects of her cleaning job. She liked the tax-free instant cash payment, flexibility, and unsupervised work autonomy—no one monitored her activity. But she also realizes she could not do such physically demanding work forever, especially as she aged: "I work at five different places five days a week. I usually get an average of $25 per hour, so I just work four to five hours a day. The money is good. I like my work because it provides me flexibility. The work hours are up to me. I can finish my work faster and still have the time to go home and fix my son snacks before he arrives. But I know that I can't do this kind of work for a long time, it's good only when I am young and strong. I can't do it after few years. I won't have physical strength and energy then."

Women's experiences in various areas of service work indicate that no particular type of service work or setting was better than another. The work conditions and labor relations differed in care and noncare work.

In both, women were rarely assigned a specific responsibility; instead, they were expected to simultaneously shoulder multiple tasks. This is because their work in the informal sector was not regulated or protected by labor laws, so employers had leverage to control the labor relations and practices.

Complex Relations: Women, Their Employers, and the Culture of Codependence

The majority of women encountered exploitative work conditions in the form of undefined labor requirements and emotional abuse. However, their labor relations should not be reduced to these forms of exploitation; women also experienced workplace relationships that were complex, intimate, and to some extent paradoxical. This was especially true for women and their South Asian employers.

Nepali women's voices reflect a culture of subtle codependency between workers and their Indian employers. As described in chapter 3, South Asian employers and employees shared close social and cultural ties. Similarities of food, language, religion (especially Hinduism), and lifestyle brought together Nepali employees and Indian employers. These ties bound them into work relations, but they also sometimes subverted the hierarchy of employer and employee. For the employers, Nepali women were specialized nannies who brought cultural capital to their jobs: they nurtured Indian employers' children with South Asian values; introduced native language, food, and culture to foreign-born children; and sometimes cooked for the entire family.

At home in Nepal, Meena had been a senior high school teacher. She was also the adviser to the principal and quite popular among her students. Meena's first job in the United States was in an Indian restaurant in Manhattan, but she worked there for only a month or so before the owner asked Meena to care for his infant son and she became a full-time nanny. For her employer, Meena was the ideal domestic worker. She shared the language and culture of her employer. She was fluent in English and Hindi and an exceptional cook. As an experienced teacher, Meena knew how to interact with children. In Meena's own words:

I understand both English and Hindi. I've tried teaching the two-year-old different languages, and that's why the parents are very impressed. I also teach different dances to the kid. Even the kid is very pleased with me. He ignores his mother and asks for me. If the kid wasn't so attached to me, then babysitting would have been very difficult for me. Older kids don't like the idea of a babysitter. They become very difficult and cry for their mother. But this kid isn't problematic. I knew how to deal with this kid. I observed what makes him happy and what makes him sad. I learned that he loves to dance. They have different kinds of music, and when I play music and pretend to dance, he becomes very happy. When he cries, and if I dance, then he becomes very curious and stops crying.

Meena's social, cultural, and professional background made her an ideal childcare provider. Her employer saw her potential to simultaneously teach and take care of his child. Meena's narrative also reflected her ability to provide maternal love and care. Meena's ability to cook was another appealing feature for her Indian employers: "I liked cooking. I'm a vegetarian and my employers are also vegetarians. I enjoyed cooking. Not everyone can prepare vegetarian meals. If they hired Spanish people then they would be nonvegetarians. I can cook vegetarian food very well because when I was in Nepal, I used to do a program on television relating to cooking. That's one of the reasons why they didn't want to let go of me, because their son got to eat good food every day."

Meena's personal and ethnic or cultural qualities made her labor both indispensable and expandable. Familiarity with South Asian food, language, and culture has brought the Indian and Nepali immigrant communities together. Although Meena seemed to be happier with her job than many other women, it is clear from the earlier accounts that these skills also make the women susceptible to labor exploitation.

The relationship between Abha and her employers illustrates similar codependencies. Abha was happy to be hired by an employer with whom she shared familiar food, religion, language, and entertainment. During the interview, she mentioned that her employers treated her like their own mother and that she considered their son (the child she takes care of) as her own grandson. In this sense, they functioned like family members:

"Today, when I was about to come here, they gave me a handbag that they bought as a gift for Mother's Day. They are very good to me. My employers own a clinic. They're both doctors. One of them is a neurologist. The other is a pediatrician. They have given me training in the clinic as well. When the clinic is very hectic I help them by taking temperatures and recording them."

Abha's quote illustrates some dualities. Abha and her employers functioned as family members, but Abha was also given training to perform tasks outside her original job description. In this context, social and labor relations were complex and ambiguous. This relationship included elements of familial support and interdependence as well as unequal labor relations with expected additional labor. When the boundaries between familial and work relations dissolved, paradoxes emerged.

Nepali women and their South Asian employers share some similar conditions and experiences as transnational workers and immigrants in the United States. Although the two groups came to the United States in different historical phases, they are both part of the South Asian diaspora. However, their social, political, and economic lives in the United States are marked by one major difference: Indians and Indian Americans are the largest financially and professionally well-established group, not only in the South Asian community but also among all ethnic minorities in the United States. As Purkayastha and Ray report, "Indians have consistently ranked among the top among all race and ethnic groups in terms of education and earnings since the 1960s . . . and the average education of Indian women and men is consistently higher than that of whites" (2010, 54).

Because of their education level and relatively long immigrant history in the United States, Indians tend to be familiar with US immigration policies and the procedures for sponsoring a permanent residency card for domestic and service labor. Because they experienced the challenges of immigration, some Indian employers were sympathetic to the immigration issues of their Nepali workers and initiated and sponsored green cards for them. Rita thus described the labor relations between Indian employers and Nepali workers in the following manner: "Whatever people say about Indians, they are the ones that mostly sponsor a green card for

Nepalese. They think that Nepalese people are hardworking and honest. We also resemble them in culture and language. So I recommend working for Indians at first. They also teach you all the work."

Indian employers were not the only employers to initiate and sponsor permanent residency for women workers. White employers expressed sympathy toward women's immigration status as well. Of the thirty-five research participants, two had obtained green cards through white American employers and three through Indian employers. In this sample, it did not appear that employers from one group or another were more willing to initiate green cards or permanent residency for women workers. Thus the women's labor conditions and labor relations did not illustrate any pattern specific to their employers' race and ethnicity. A shared culture as part of the South Asian diaspora brought together Nepali women workers and their South Asian employers, but their work experiences and labor relations remained paradoxical. Similarities of cultural ties, immigration experience, and membership in a regional diasporic community were missing from the relationships among white employers, but this did not mean the women's work conditions and labor relations were different or worse in those households.

A few women worked for both Indian and white families. Their descriptions of these employers were mixed:

> Americans really value your hard work a lot and also see how reliable you are. If they like you, they will give you a raise and will treat you better.

> But I'll tell you one thing. It is the Indians who help us out. By giving us jobs at first, they give us a chance. Even if they don't have vacancies, they will find a job for us in their friend's gas station, convenience store, or restaurant. They use their connections and they don't ask for references.

> One of the differences between working for an American employer and an Indian employer is that an American employer will pay your salary even if they are on vacation. But an Indian will not pay you when they are not around.

> It really does not matter whether the employer is an Indian or a white. What matters is their education and how civilized they are. I worked

for an Indian couple for a long time; they were very nice people. They respected me, they paid me on time, everything was going well. But when her mother came from India, she would constantly watch me and would give me tasks. She had this mindset that I should not take a break at all. When I would take a break or sit for some time, she would come and would look at me in a way that would signal her disapproval. She would tell me what needs to be cleaned or done. She treated me as though I was a servant. Her daughter and son-in-law were completely different though. They are educated and nice people. They treated me well.

The women's labor experiences indicated no clear advantages in the work conditions offered by employers of one particular race or nationality. Indians employed most of the research participants, which limits a broad comparison of women's labor relations with non-South Asian employers. Nevertheless, it is clear that sociocultural relations between the women and their Indian employers led to contradictory labor relations. Such relations at times blurred the delicate balance between work and familial roles and paid and unpaid work. The absence of a firm line to demarcate women workers as family members or laborers complicated their relationship. On the one hand, the South Asian sociocultural ties expanded job opportunities to women in a homelike environment. But on the other hand, these associations intensified the workload. The women's South Asian networks were thus a source of abuse as well as support.

Conclusion

This chapter addressed four main issues: (1) the pitfalls of work in informal domestic and service sectors; (2) women's work conditions and positions in the labor market vis-à-vis their race, class, gender, nationality, and immigration status; (3) women's work experiences in care and non-care work; and (4) paradoxical labor relationship between Nepali women and their South Asian Indian employers in ethnically segmented labor markets.

Women encountered labor exploitation, emotional abuse, and marginalization in the informal labor market. Although some were attracted to the informal sector for its perks, they quickly recognized its pitfalls.

Women faced a series of personal and professional challenges while working a long day and night in service, domestic, and care work.

The women's employment patterns and experiences in coethnic households illustrate interesting dynamics. Several participants indicated that Indians open a door for Nepalis by providing jobs in the coethnic informal labor market. Women also revealed that they and their Indian employers were drawn to each other because of shared aspects of their cultures. However, common membership in the South Asian diaspora did not eliminate exploitative labor conditions. Whether women worked for a white family or coethnic family, they encountered unfair work conditions that led to exploitation and emotional abuse. Nor did employers' level of education and professionalism automatically mean better work conditions; women experienced labor and emotional abuse in households where the employers were professionals such as doctors and software engineers. In the case of women working for Indian employers, exploitative labor conditions intensified when the boundary blurred between being perceived as a family member or as a worker.

The labor conditions and labor relations between South Asian employers and employees are particularly complex and full of dualities. Cultural similarities, shared membership in the South Asian diaspora, and national and regional identity are important elements that bring together South Asian employers and employees. Some of the narratives clearly indicate that Nepali women wanted to work for Indian families because of their shared food, language, religion, and popular culture. Similarly, Indian employers sought out Nepali women because they could speak Hindi and read the Devanagari script, shared cultural values, and were perceived as good mothers. These elements did not automatically prevent labor exploitation or emotional abuse, however. Unequal power relations between employees and employers co-opted these social and cultural ties and gave employers the authority to demand limitless and unspecified work. Conflict arose when workers encountered economic and emotional exploitation and abuse. Exploitation included cases where a childcare provider was expected to be a domestic, where workers were accused of stealing, and where workers encountered prejudice based on their Nepali nationality and perceived lower socioeconomic status.

An intersectional analysis reveals that women's immigration status, nationality, citizenship, race, ethnicity, gender, and social class led to marginalization and exploitation in the workplace. No single factor was more crucial than another in generating oppression; rather, these factors operated together to create an interlocking system of oppression and exploitation that generates combined effects. Within the intersections of gender, ethnicity, cultural background, nationality, and immigration status, female domestic and service workers in the informal labor market became ideal workers as well as victims. These were the paradoxes of the women's work lives.

US immigration policy is designed to serve men as the primary immigrants. Kelkar reports that "men and women experience immigration in very different ways" (2011, 55). In general, immigration policies are meant to serve those who live, study, or work in the United States legally. Most women in this book worked in the invisible, informal, and highly feminized service sectors because they did not have legal authorization to work. Nepali women thus fit into US immigration policy.[5]

In terms of a cross-national comparison, Nepali women's labor experiences were no different from those of Latina, Caribbean, African American, and Chicana domestics reported in the work of Hondagneu-Sotelo (2007), Rollins (1985), and Romero (1992). Common denominators such as gender, race, ethnicity, nationality, and citizenship status make them highly vulnerable to labor exploitation and emotional abuse. But these are the same factors that make immigrant women the preferred source of labor in the informal service and domestic sectors, enabling them to access jobs when other more formal work is closed to them. A paradox emerges when the marginalization of informal workers is enabled by the very factors that bring them into these sectors in the first place.

---

5. Men were not part of this study. Hence, we will not be able to analyze and determine how women and men would experience immigration differently in the informal or illegal work domain. In chapter 5 I discuss the ramifications of women's immigration status in their parental and conjugal relationships.

The women's narratives mirrored some distinctive patterns of women's work and the informal economic world. First, nearly all of the women hired specifically to provide childcare were ultimately required to cook, clean, and perform other domestic duties. Second, some women combined childcare with other informal work such as restaurant or convenience store work. Third, those who initially began work as childcare providers switched back and forth with informal economic work (i.e., restaurant and convenience store work). Fourth, as women became experienced childcare providers and when they established themselves in the service sectors, they looked for better-paying jobs elsewhere. Women who gained a legal immigration and work status had even stronger bargaining power. With years of work experience and legal status, women could freely negotiate their wage and work conditions. Fifth, experienced women acted as the main point of contact for employers and employees. As they gained years of work experience in the United States, these women became the main sources of employment for friends, relatives, and new migrants/immigrants in the community. In many cases, women recruited others as their own replacements when they moved on to better-paying jobs.[6] Employers relied on these women's informal social networks to find a suitable care or service worker. Women's social networks and transnational ties manifested in this context and their transnational connections and cultural capital have remained vital sources of employment. Experienced workers become the main recruiters trusted by employers and employees alike, providing a continuum of carework in the informal work sector.

6. New migrants tended to work for South Asian families first. Even when they changed employers, many continued working for coethnic employers. This pattern is different from Hondagneu-Sotelo's (2001) study; domestic workers in her study often preferred to work for whites than for ethnic minorities. A few women used their first jobs as a starting point for entry into other service work in non-coethnic households.

5

o   o   o

Shifting Gender Roles in Private and Public Domains

Immigration, Migration, and Transnational Family Dynamics

My husband tries to work. . . . but he does not sustain in any job for more than a few months. He does not like to do manual labor. . . . He is not used to this type of work, I mean cleaning and doing dishes. . . . More than anything, I think he does not like to be ill-treated.

—Live-in childcare provider in Boston

MIGRATING TO THE UNITED STATES did not simply change Nepali women's work lives; it also altered their personal, family, and community lives. When Nepali women became transnational workers, they faced downward occupational mobility into low-paying and low-status jobs in the United States, but many also became the main source of income for their families. Women's new breadwinner status changed the dynamics of relations between husbands and wives and between mothers and children.

In this chapter, I analyze how women's migration to the United States and their paid work affected their position within and outside their family and community. In particular, I focus on how the interplay of gender, labor, and migration produced changes in women's personal, conjugal, and family lives. I begin the chapter with a brief discussion of gender ideologies and expectations in Nepal. I review pertinent studies related to the dynamics of gender as it intersects with caste, ethnicity, and social class. I then turn to the women's narratives to discuss how becoming a

84

transnational worker altered women's status in the family. I discuss how family members responded to women's decision to migrate and work transnationally and how women's remittances affected family life. As women's transnational work enhanced their personal autonomy and decision-making power in the family, their new contributions sometimes conflicted with traditional gender norms, creating both contradictions and new opportunities to reshape gender relations in the family.

Intersections of Gender, Caste, Ethnicity, and Class in Nepal

Historically, particularly since the era of state formation, the state reinforced a patriarchal system that influences relations within families and in the broader society. During the period of state formation, a patriarchal code of conduct was incorporated into the state's cultural, social, political, economic, and legal structures and systems, resulting in women's oppression, subordination, and exploitation. Centuries of gendered oppression, violence, and inequality gave rise to a women's movement during the era of the People's Movement in the 1990s. According to Bhadra, "The political, social, economic and legal marginalization of women and the pervading violence against women became the igniting force for the women's movement in early 1990s" (2009, 80).[1] Advocacy and pressure groups that emerged as part of the women's movement demanded women's civil, political, economic, and human rights. Bhadra notes, "The more the patriarchal resistance, the stronger became the women's movement to the extent of women taking to the streets in large numbers" (2009, 80).

The women's movement was very successful in making women's issues visible, demanding women's rights, and improving women's sociocultural, political, and economic status in Nepal. However, many Nepali women still encounter gender-based discrimination and inequalities in their everyday lives. Poverty, violence, illiteracy, sexual exploitation, and labor exploitation all remain heavily feminized in Nepal, particularly among the rural and urban poor and among migrants. Other inequalities

---

1. See Bhadra (2009) for an in-depth discussion of the women's movement in Nepal and its effects.

of caste, ethnicity, class, and region exacerbate gender-based inequality and discrimination.

Nepali women's gendered experiences are not uniform in this multiethnic, multilingual, and multicultural nation. Caste, ethnicity, social class, and regional locations shape their experiences. Although Nepal as a patriarchal state has shaped the political economy of gender and gender ideologies in a broader national context, the degree of patriarchy varies according to caste, ethnicity, class, and region. As Tamang puts it, "To take the most well-known examples, orthodox Hindu groups emphasize the sexual purity of women; Thakali and Sherpa communities take pride in the business acumen and marketing abilities of their females; and Tibetan-origin groups inhabiting the northern rimland of Nepal practice polyandrous marriage" (2002, 162). Larger structural conditions such as the national political economy, the development process, and economic restructuring disrupt customary gender practices and ideologies among ethnic and tribal communities. During the state formation process in the eighteenth century—when Hinduism became the state religion—most of the Gurung (Tibeto-Burman ethnic group) people in Tebas village (situated in the midhill region of Nepal) followed the norms and values of Hinduism and were concerned about "purity" and "pollution" (McHugh, 1989). Among the Dolpo people, Fisher reports that "the sense of pollution is even stricter and more powerful—and prohibition against it even stronger—than in traditional Hindu culture" (1986, 161). Changes in caste and ethnic-based values in turn bring changes in gender ideology and relations.

Scholars who have studied the positions of Nepali women in relation to caste, ethnicity, and social class have shown different gendered patterns. In their classic study, Acharaya and Bennett (1981) suggest that the higher the caste, the more rigid and oppressive the social system is for women. Studies indicate that gender relations among non-Hindu communities and low-caste groups are more egalitarian than in high-caste Hindu communities (Acharya and Bennett 1981; Watkins 1995; Furer-Haimendorf 1964; Subedi 1993). These studies also suggest that women in non-Hindu groups have more decision-making power than high-caste Hindu women and participate widely in the market economy. High-caste women may experience more oppression owing to strict patriarchal gender norms and household gender relations. However, because of the historical legacy of the caste hierarchy, high-caste women often have relatively more access to education and resources as well as extensive sociopolitical ties. Similarly, although freedom of movement and decision-making powers are greater among lower-caste women, these factors do not automatically free women from other structural inequalities.

The effects of caste, ethnicity, gender, and class are not frozen in time and space; instead, these factors affect women differently in different stages of the nation's political history and of women's individual biographies. For example, a study conducted by the Center for Governance indicated that women's household economic condition—rather than their caste—was the primary factor determining their labor mobility. Cameron (1998) and Hamal Gurung (2003) also reported that women's paid work intersected with gender, caste, and social class to improve women's position in society.

Making a Transnational Family: Crossing Borders, Visa Categories, and Immigration Policies

A transnational family is one in which family members live in more than one country. Macro-level structural conditions such as international migratory circuits and host nations' immigration policies combine with micro-level factors in migrants' personal and social lives to create such families. In recent years, transnational family structures have become a prominent feature of migrants' lives around the globe. Migrant women—rather than men—typically take a leading role in forming and maintaining transnational families (Zontini 2004; Parreñas 2005; Hondagneu-Sotelo 2007; Gamburd 2008).

Most of the women in this book initially came to the United States alone on a visitor or business visa. A few came with their husbands and children—this was particularly true in the cases where the woman or her husband had won the DV lottery. Most of those who came to the United States alone were still living apart from their husbands and children. Some of these women had acquired permanent residency ("green card" status) through work sponsorship or political asylum. In such cases, their husbands and children were often in the process of joining them or had already done so. However, even after a woman obtains a green card, not all of her family members are automatically eligible for permanent residency, especially if her children are over twenty-one. In two cases in this study, the age criterion prevented children from joining their families in the United States. By default, immigration policies contributed to their family separation.

In some cases, women were able to live on and off with their husbands or children even without acquiring permanent residency. This was particularly true for those whose husbands could obtain visitor visas to visit their wives. However, in the majority of such cases, for various cultural, social, or legal reasons, the husbands did not permanently remain in the United States. Similarly, some women were able to live with their children because the children were already studying in the United States or had come later to study. Nonetheless, most of the women were living apart from their immediate family members, including their children and husbands.

Transnational Workers: Spatial Separation and Transnationalizing Mothering

Feminist and transnational studies of gendered migration and transnational mothers show that transnational families face complex dilemmas in both local and global contexts (Da 2010; Gamburd 2008; Hondagneu-Sotelo 2007; Hondagneu-Sotelo and Avila 1997; Parreñas 2005). When a wife and mother is the head migrant, traditional gendered family dynamics are destabilized, requiring a reconfiguration of gender relations in the family. Feminist studies of migrant mothers show that motherhood is historically and socially constructed (Dill 1992; Zinn 1994; Hondagneu-Sotelo 2007; Hondagneu-Sotelo and Avila 1997; Gamburd 2008). Structural factors shape the meaning of motherhood for migrant women as well as the social and emotional experiences of mothers and their children. Long-term spatial separation between mothers and children may create conflict or emotional distance, but children also recognize the importance of their mother's economic contribution (Gamburd 2008; Parreñas 2005). Faced with the structural challenges to traditional mothering practices, immigrant/migrant women workers strategically engage in long-distance mothering through technology (Hondagneu-Sotelo and Avila 1997; Parreñas 2005).

Similar to other transnational mothers, the Nepali women participants in this book struggled emotionally with the physical separation from their children (Romero 1992, 2006; Hondagneu-Sotelo 2007; Hondagneu-Sotelo and Avila 1997; Lan 2006; Gamburd 2008). Many women expressed the desire to have greater contact with their children by bringing them to the United States. But various social, political, economic, and legal factors restricted their options, making transnational mothering a long-term project.

Manju, a forty-one-year-old childcare provider, came to Boston in 2008 after the Maoists killed her husband. His death left Manju alone to care for their daughter. Because of the political nature of her husband's death, she felt insecure in Nepal. She said: "My husband was a pretty well-known person in his town and the Maoists really wanted him to join their political party. But he didn't like it at all, so he became a target. So they eventually killed him. If my husband were alive, I probably wouldn't be here today. When they killed him, I didn't feel safe to live there. My daughter is in Nepal, and my objective right now is to get her here soon. I am worried about her safety."

With the help of family and friends, Manju came to the United States alone, leaving her daughter with her parents in Nepal. At the time of our interview, she had initiated the paperwork for political asylum to try to sponsor her daughter to migrate as well. Manju is hopeful that her case will be approved and that her daughter will join her soon. Even if her case is approved, because of the lengthy and complex immigration and visa process, it may be several years before her daughter can come to the United States. If her case is not approved, Manju will continue to be a transnational mother as her daughter grows up. In either situation, the mother and daughter will have to live apart for a long time.

The majority of the women in this book were mothers. Some had older children, some younger. Regardless of their children's ages, all of the women were constantly engaged in transnational mothering. As was the case for migrant domestic workers from Mexico and Central America (Hondagneu-Sotelo and Avila 1997) and Sri Lanka (Gamburd 2003), the physical separation from their children was challenging and emotionally draining. Hondagneu-Sotelo and Avila (1997) eloquently capture the dilemmas faced by transnational mothers:

> The ties of transnational motherhood simultaneously suggest the relative permeability of borders, as witnessed by the maintenance of family ties and the new meanings of motherhood, and the impermeability of nation-state borders. Ironically, just at the moment when free trade proponents and pundits celebrate globalization and transnationalism, and when "borderlands" and "border crossings" have become the metaphors of preference for describing a mind-boggling range of conditions, nation-state borders prove to be very real obstacles for many Mexican and Central American women who work in the United States and who, given the appropriate circumstances, wish to be with their children. (1997, 268)

Nearly every mother in this study indicated that transnational family arrangements harmed her ability to mother and that she longed to be with her children. Like other transnational mothers, Nepali women provided love, care, and support to their children through phone calls, e-mails, gifts, and remittances. When they finished a long day or night of paid care work, women began their second shift providing long-distance mothering to their biological children. Women indicated that they often called home to Nepal between 9 p.m. and 6 a.m. when cell phone minutes were free. Through phone calls, e-mail, Instant Messaging, Skype, and other forms of social media, women expressed affection for their children, offered advice, and participated in decision-making regarding their care.

In addition to regular communication over the phone, Internet, or through social media, women also sent remittance money back to Nepal to support their children economically and showered their children with expensive gifts. Long-distance communication and financial support could not fully substitute for their physical presence in their children's lives, however. Physical separation took a significant toll on the emotional and psychological well-being of mothers and children alike, especially among younger children. In her study of undocumented Salvadoran working mothers in the United States, Horton (2009) reports that mothers experienced a feeling of moral failure, powerlessness, and emotional trauma when they could not reunite with their children within their expected time frame. Children also resented their mothers or pleaded that they return home. Likewise, the mothers and children in this study experienced some emotional and psychological harm as a result of their separation. For example, Tara lamented: "I haven't seen my children for five years. They were very young when I left. They were ten, eleven years old. Now when I see their photographs, I can't even recognize them. They've changed so much. They've grown so much. I call [my children] almost every day, sometimes twice a day. . . . If I don't hear their voices, then I will go crazy. I called them this morning to wake them up because they have their exams going on right now. . . . I am physically here, but I am mentally with my kids all the time."

According to Tara, her children were equally concerned about her well-being: "I was very sick on Mother's Day and I had to be hospitalized. My son told me that he had nightmares about me getting hurt so he told me to come back. He said that if we are together, then we can get through all the hurdles in life together. I really want to see them."

Although physical separation caused pain and suffering, mothers recognized the importance of a good education and a better life for their children. Single mothers in particular were working hard in the United States so their children could attend elite private schools in Nepal or abroad.[2] All the mothers hoped to bring their children to the United States one day, particularly to provide a US education that would provide greater job prospects, economic security, and personal security.

There is no single definition of what constitutes a "good mother." Do migrant women's economic contributions make them good mothers? Do

---

2. In Nepal, parents invest in their children's education. The concept of student loans or a student paying for their own college education is nonexistant. Some public schools are available, but private schools are viewed as better in quality. It is common for parents to make sacrifices for their children's education. Even for middle- and upper-middle-class families, it is costly to send their children abroad or to a technical or medical school. A US education is a dream for many parents and children. Because women saw that their migration could make such an education possible, they prioritized their children's education over their physical separation and emotional distress.

their sacrifices compensate for physical separation? Scholars who have examined these issues have reported that despite women's valuable economic contributions and capital investment in their children's well-being, they encounter criticism and resentment for leaving their children behind (Anderson 2006; Hondagneu-Sotelo and Avila 1997; Gamburd 2005; Romero 2006). Many societies idealize women's nurturing and care work. Thus transnational mothers actively employ various strategies to fulfill their motherly responsibilities. In doing so, they "reconstitute mothering by providing acts of care from afar, but also often do so by overcompensating for their physical absence and performing a transnational version of what Sharon Hays (1996) identifies as 'intensive mothering'"(Parreñas 2005, 323).

Previous studies of Filipino, Latino, and Sri Lankan migrant mothers have examined women who became domestic laborers because of economic struggles at home. In all of these cases, migrant women were often criticized for being away from their children. In the case of the many Nepali migrant women participants in this book, low family socioeconomic status was not the motivating factor behind their migration and domestic labor in the United States; instead, they were motivated by social, cultural, and personal reasons. In stark contrast to previous studies, the Nepali women migrants I interviewed did not report facing criticism for being away from their children.[3]

Like other migrant mothers, most Nepali women in this book were the main income earners in their families. Similar to other transnational mothers, Nepali women migrants also relied on kin to take care of their children back home. Rather than employ professional caregivers, Nepali women migrants enlisted the help of mothers, husbands, mothers-in-law, sisters, brothers, and sisters-in-law to take care of their children. Unlike cases of migrants from lower socioeconomic backgrounds, these family members were often supported in their care by domestic workers. In some cases, children also lived away from their relatives at private boarding schools.

---

3. Instead, their family and friends asked them to stay in the United States to provide for their children's future.

By performing productive and reproductive work simultaneously, Nepali women prioritized their children's social and economic well-being with a great sense of moral obligation and economic responsibility. They navigated personal, local, and global resources and employed various strategies in being and remaining a good mother.

Gendered Labor, Gendered Ideologies, and Conjugal Relationships in Transnational Family

Mothering was not the only relationship transformed by Nepali women's transnational migration; women's conjugal relationships were also negotiated across a transnational context. When women became migrant workers in the United States, their move disrupted the spatial living arrangements that are often taken for granted in marital relationships. In addition, their work and income in the United States disrupted the male breadwinner model, requiring husbands and wives to shift their gendered expectations of each other's contributions to the marriage.

Five of the women participants originally migrated to the United States with their husbands. Whereas these Nepali women migrants engaged in informal income-generating activities, their husbands were not able to do so for multiple reasons. First, employers in the informal and service sectors—particularly in domestic and care work—do not favor men, so it was more difficult for husbands to find jobs in these sectors. In these sectors, Nepali women were viewed as "ideal" workers. As migrants, their unauthorized work status required that they accept work in the informal economy. As South Asians, their pan-coethnic employers prized their cultural attributes. And as women, their experience performing unpaid reproductive labor was easily transferred from the private sphere in Nepal into semi-public paid work in the transnational arena.

Few Nepali men were motivated to work in these sectors. In Nepali society, women perform most paid and unpaid reproductive work. A gendered cultural ideology prevails in which reproductive labor is viewed as "women's work." Thus, upon migration to the United States, many Nepali migrant husbands were unmotivated to engage in informal service or domestic work. Although many professional Nepali women, as women, also did not see this type of work as ideal they were more willing to work in these sectors to meet their social, economic, political, and familial goals. Although exploitative work conditions and oppressive labor relations led some women to quit their immediate jobs, they continued to work in the informal sectors.

Finally, some women supported the traditional gender division of labor. Three participants directly stated and two others indirectly implied that their husbands should not take jobs in the informal or service sectors. Instead, they thought their husbands should have office jobs. Because such formal jobs are harder for Nepali migrants to find than informal jobs, women became the primary breadwinners in the United States.

Instead of working in low-status service and informal sectors, some husbands preferred to return to Nepal. The husbands of three participants went back to Nepal while their wives remained in New York City and Boston; the husbands of two others traveled back and forth. In these two cases, the husbands and wives formulated this arrangement because of immigration issues and the husbands' higher-status jobs in Nepal. In the other three, when the wives realized their husbands were not happy, could not survive in service-sector jobs, or would not be able to get office jobs, they did not stop their husbands from going home.

Whereas the women were willing to give up their professional jobs, their husbands did not want to relinquish their professional occupations for low-status jobs in the United States. In such cases, the husbands worked in Nepal and visited their families in the United States once a year or every few years. When they visited, they would stay a few months.

This was the family arrangement of Kabita's household.

Kabita, her husband, and their children immigrated to the United States after her husband won the DV lottery. But he returned to Nepal because he was an established attorney there. Although he continued to support Kabita and the children financially and visit them as much as possible, Kabita was the head of her household in the United States. She made all household decisions, including those concerning her children's education. She managed household's finances and was responsible for allocating and distributing resources in and outside her household.

Syama is another participant whose husband lives and works in Nepal. Syama had lived and worked in the Boston area since 2004. Her husband came to the United States on a B2 (tourist) visa twice; both times, he stayed with Syama for two months before returning to Nepal. His respectable job back home made it easy to obtain a US visitor visa. Syama's narrative illustrates a combination of immigration, sociocultural, and gender factors that contributed to her transnational family arrangement and conjugal relationship. During my follow-up interview with Syama in the summer of 2009, she shared:

> My husband came to America twice and we were together for some time. When he was here, we discussed whether he should work and live in America. He wanted to try, so my friends helped us find a job for him. He began work in an Indian grocery store but then quit because he was asked to clean the toilet and mop the floor. He found the work and life-style in America challenging. He was not used to doing any household chores. My working hours were longer, so most of the time he was alone in the apartment and getting bored. So, when the duration of his visitor visa was ending, we had to decide about his plan. He had a respect[able] job in Nepal . . . and he was definitely not happy with the job situation here. And with his visa status, it was impossible to find him a decent job. My current immigration status doesn't help the situation either. If he had stayed here, he would have been out of status and it would not have been good for him to stay that way. So we decided that he should go back to Nepal. When I get a green card, he will come back and stay with me.

Syama's husband lived and worked in Nepal, but encouraged her to stay and work in the United States. He told Syama to try to get permanent residency and planned to come to the United States after she obtained this status. Syama's employers had processed paperwork for her green card, but it could take several years for the government to approve her application. This means that her conjugal relationship could remain transnational for an indefinite period of time.

Although Syama was a senior nurse and social worker in Nepal, unlike her husband, she did not shy away from work in the service and care sectors as an undocumented worker. Professionally, she encountered significant downward mobility and experienced many challenges and hardships. Nonetheless, in her narrative of her husband's work, immigration status, and lifestyle in the United States, it appeared that her husband's challenges were more important than hers. By placing her own struggles as secondary to her husband's, Syama enacted a form of patriarchy even as her position as the primary breadwinner and head of household in the United States challenged traditional patriarchal marital relationships. Thus Nepali women's transnational conjugal arrangements produced gendered contradictions.

For couples that first migrated to the United States together, husbands were less inclined than their wives to work in informal sector jobs and deal with work- and immigration-related hurdles. But they encouraged their wives to work and live in the United States and create a legal way for them to return. Another Boston-based childcare provider whose husband left for Nepal because of work-related issues stated:

> My husband used to work in an Indian restaurant. He always complained about his work. I would tell him to be patient and tolerant. He was not happy about the nature of his job. He found the job physically demanding and exhausting. He had to lift heavy stuff, wash the dishes, and clean. He was also not accustomed to people yelling at him at work. He was not used to being dominated. I told him to just simply discard such things and carry on. He was really getting frustrated though, so I told him to go back to Nepal. He went back, and I stayed behind. When things get better, he will come back.

Nitu provides an example of a migrant worker who was on her way to fulfilling the goal of creating a pathway for her husband to migrate and find a job in the formal market. Nitu, a forty-six-year-old childcare provider and restaurant worker, came to the United States for the first time in 1998 with her husband. He primarily worked in restaurants and gas stations, jobs that he hated. He did not last in any job in the United States for more than three months. He became emotionally distressed, and Nitu was concerned about his social and emotional well-being. After a year, they returned to Nepal.

Later, in 2005, Nitu returned to the United States by herself and became a restaurant worker and childcare provider. Her husband did not want to return to the difficult work conditions he previously faced in the

United States, so Nitu migrated alone this time. Nitu found work in the informal economy and her employers sponsored permanent residency. At the time of our interview, Nitu was in the final stages of obtaining a green card; her husband planned to return to the United States as soon as she obtained permanent residency.

Transnational families' new arrangements occur within a broader context of globalization, feminization of migration and the labor force, immigration and visa policies, and gender ideologies. Other studies illustrate how structural barriers in the host nations can create transnational conjugal relationships during the settlement process. Zontini (2004) reports that the Moroccan women migrants to Barcelona she studied were not able to reach their goal of reuniting with their husbands because their involvement in domestic service meant that many women "lived in" with their employers or lacked family housing. She stated that for the women she studied, a lack of adequate housing meant that women migrants were "forced by legal impediments to live in a transnational household" (1123).

In addition to the issue of housing for women working in domestic service, Da (2010) highlighted professional and occupational policies as a source of marital conflict and tension. When her migrant research participants' and their husbands' educational credentials and occupational backgrounds in China were not accepted in Canada, both husbands and wives had to either go to a Canadian college or university or take a job beneath their qualification. This produced financial constraints and struggles over childcare responsibilities that put some marriages into "crisis" (538).

Transnational families are characterized by geographically scattered family members, long-distance conjugal relationships, and familial conflict. In addition, many transnational families depend on wives' and mothers' income and remittances for their household economies, the children's well-being, and transnational community building. This economic factor alters power relations between husbands and wives, leading to a shift in gender relations in private and public spheres.

Shifting Family and Household Gender Relations

In the new globalized labor market for service and care work, women are favored as workers because of their association with unpaid reproductive work and because of their skills in this area. But the economic demand for women's labor is not the only factor shaping the transnational family arrangements of migrant workers; other structural factors, including gender immigration policies and gender socialization, also produce contradictions that simultaneously support and subvert traditional gender relations.

Most of the women in this book were working professionals in Nepal but were not the primary jobholders or breadwinners in their families. Their income was considered supplemental to their household economies. However, in the United States, many of them—regardless of whether they migrated alone or with their husbands—became the main income earners for their families.

Ironically, the participants' US-based lower-status informal sector work generated more money than their professional work in Nepal. First, because the value of the US dollar was higher than the Nepalese rupee (one US dollar was equivalent to about seventy-two Nepalese rupees at the time of the research, 2005–9), women's low-wage earnings converted into higher wages in Nepal. Second, for husbands and wives that migrated together, whereas the women continued to work and earn in the informal service sector, their husbands did not last in such jobs. Finally, the women had longer work weeks in the United States than in Nepal, working twelve hours a day, six to seven days a week. For these reasons, migrant women's earnings in the United States often surpassed even those of their husbands who were working professionals back home.

For the many participants who were single mothers, separated wives, or widows, their remittances were even more critical for their families' sustenance and children's well-being. These women financed 100 percent of their children's education and upbringing. For example, when Tara's husband abandoned her and their children for another woman, Tara became solely responsible for her children's social and financial well-being. Her teaching job in Nepal was not adequate to cover her children's private school expenses. Through her childcare work in the United States, Tara was able to send her children to a prestigious private boarding school back home and provide for their other economic needs. Her brother and sister-in-law were her children's guardians in Nepal. Her dissolved conjugal relationship precipitated her move to the United States, but this move ultimately allowed her to provide for her children beyond what her husband had been able to contribute in Nepal.

As a single mother, Gina was the sole source of financial support for her teenage daughter in the United States. Gina initially came to the United States because of the media attention and social humiliation she faced as an unwed mother. After migrating, Gina became the sole breadwinner for her family.

Nira, a forty-three-year-old New York-based convenience store worker, came to the United States when her husband moved in with another woman and stopped supporting Nira and their son financially. In Nepal, Nira was an NGO worker, but the income from her NGO work did not cover her son's private school tuition and other household expenditures. With the help of her social network, she came to the United States and began working in the informal sector. Like Tara and Gina, Nira became the sole provider for her son's education and financial well-being. Even those women who were not single mothers sent a large portion of their earnings back home. Their remittances were allocated to their children's education, capital investment in family property, and cash gifts to family members.

Power Relations at the Crossroads of Labor and Gender: Nepal Context

Studies of Nepali women show that women's paid work has positive social and economic effects for the women and their families. Bhadra discusses the positive impact of Nepali female migrants' economic contribution to various aspects of their lives, reporting that "migration and remittances have increased women's self-esteem by bringing about a positive change in their gender identity and relations, leading to a decrease in violence against women and an increase in love and respect among the family and community" (Bhadra 2007, 2). Cameron (1998) also reports that low-caste women's increasing participation in paid work has improved the socioeconomic condition of their homes and communities. During previous research on factory- and home-based carpet production in Nepal (Hamal Gurung 2003), I surveyed women about the impact of their wages on their family and personal lives. Of the hundred women I surveyed, seventy-four responded that migration had improved their families' socioeconomic conditions and eighty-one indicated that their wage work or income had raised their families' standard of living. Furthermore, seventy-eight of the women said their income participation had positively changed their position in the family. This finding echoes Bhadra's statement that "working females are empowered by being the major breadearner in the family" (1997, 28).

In accordance with these studies, the narratives of participants in this book also suggest that their income affected their lives in a positive manner. Women's new economic roles enhanced their decision-making power as they decided where, when, and how to spend or distribute their income. Although informal economic work was professionally degrading, the money earned through these jobs allowed women to invest in cultural, social, and economic transnationalism. This, in turn, enabled them to achieve respect and status on familial, societal, national, international, and transnational levels. The following sections specifically analyze how these women's new economic roles in the United States reversed traditional gendered expectations and shifted conjugal power relations.

Transnational Family and Power Dynamics: Wives, Husbands, and Conjugal Relationships

In this section, I discuss gender relations and power dynamics among the families where husbands and wives both lived in the United States. Like the women whose husbands came to the United States only to return to Nepal, husbands had a more difficult time finding and keeping jobs in the informal service sectors. Even when husbands found jobs in convenience stores or restaurants, they tended to quit and change their jobs quite frequently. In other words, husbands were mobile workers who worked on and off, whereas the wives held steady jobs and were the main income earners.[4] This subverted traditional gendered labor dynamics

---

4. Even if husbands lasted in such jobs, it harmed their social well-being and emotional health. Although wives also changed their jobs owing to exploitative work conditions, they took other jobs right away. They did not stay home without earning an income.

between spouses. Because women worked long hours to generate an income, some husbands cooked meals and performed housework. Thus although some husbands were reluctant to earn an income from so-called feminized service and informal sector work outside their household, they were involved in performing the same traditionally perceived women's work in their home.

What is most compelling about this shift is that the husbands did not mind doing unpaid reproductive tasks in the home. The shift indicates immigrants' response to a new lifestyle in the United States as well as the relaxing of patriarchal gender ideologies. Changing work and family life in the United States required Nepali husbands' participation in household tasks. Their reluctance to do similar jobs outside the home may be because they did not want to be publicly seen as performing low-status service or reproductive tasks. Immigration and migration to the United States thus brought Nepali wives into paid work in public and semi-public arenas and husbands into nonpaid household work in private arenas.

Rama was a thirty-nine-year-old childcare provider who lived with her husband in New York. While she was at work, her husband did the cooking and other household tasks. He even cooked during the weekends. I asked Rama whether he was used to cooking and doing household work in Nepal, and she replied,

> No, he never cooked and cleaned back home. He sometimes made tea, that's all. The men, especially in the middle-class and upper-middle-class households, rarely do any cooking, cleaning, or household work. Usually, the women are responsible for household tasks. In a joint family, there is a mother, wife, sisters, and daughters who are in charge of household tasks. In a nuclear family, if a wife has a job, then there will be a helper [maid or other servant] to do the household tasks. So you see that the man is not required or expected to do any of the household work. . . . But here, men don't have those kinds of options. I work long days, and we can't afford to keep a helper. Here, I myself work like a helper. Although I am hired as a childcare provider, I also do other household work such as cooking and cleaning. My husband gradually learned how to cook and do other household work. Sometimes I need to

stay overnight at my work, and if he doesn't cook, he will stay hungry. My work situation and our lifestyle in America have in a way forced him to learn cooking, cleaning, and other household work. Now they have become his normal chores; he cooks and cleans even during the weekend and when I am at home.

Kanti's case was somewhat similar to Rama's. Kanti was a fifty-year-old live-in childcare provider who came to Boston with her husband in 2007. While she worked as a live-in nanny in the suburbs, her husband worked in an Indian convenience store in Boston. Her job generated more income than her husband's. Kanti and her husband shared an apartment with another Nepali family. During the week, Kanti stayed at her employer's house; she returned to her apartment on Friday evenings and left again on Sundays. Her work life and her living and working arrangement changed the gendered distribution of labor in the household.

On Friday evenings, Kanti's husband went grocery shopping, prepared dinner, and eagerly awaited Kanti's arrival. When she arrived home, they ate together. On Saturdays and Sundays, her husband tried to cook the food Kanti liked and do most of the household tasks. When asked if he always participated in cooking and cleaning back home, Kanti replied: "Not really, and there was no need of this. Back home, I did most of the cooking, and we also had a helper who did washing and cleaning. Now, since I am a live-in babysitter, he does everything. When I come home during the weekend, he won't let me do the housework and cooking. He says that I should rest. He is not like a typical Nepali husband. He really supports me. He knows that my work is important for our future and for our family's economy."

Maya also lived with her husband in New York. Her job was full time and stable; her husband worked part time, on and off. Often, Maya worked weekends. This schedule shifted the gendered distribution of labor in their household. Similar to Rama's and Kanti's cases, while Maya was at work, her husband did the grocery shopping, cooked, and cleaned the house. Even when Maya was home, her husband did the cooking and cleaning.

Whereas Rama and Kanti came from traditional Hindu families and Chettri ethnic backgrounds, Maya came from the Tibeto-Burman ethnic community. A few studies have indicated that gender relations are more egalitarian in Tibeto-Burman (ethnic minorities) than in Indo-Aryan (high caste and ethnic) Hindu communities (Acharya and Bennett 1981; Watkins 1995; Subedi 1993). Thus when Maya discussed this division of labor, I assumed that she might have experienced a more egalitarian arrangement in Nepal as well. However, when I asked how she and her husband divided chores in Nepal, this is how Maya described their household duties: "When we were in Nepal, I did not work outside of home at all. I only took care of the house, children, and family affairs. My day would start with cooking and cleaning. My husband was the economic provider of the family. He would leave home around 9 a.m. after breakfast and would come back around 6 p.m. After dinner, when I would get busy cleaning the dishes and sweeping the floor, my husband would usually go out and hang around with his friends. He never participated in cooking or helping me in other household tasks. He was very carefree."

When I asked Maya when and how he started to cook and clean, she replied: "After we moved here, he picked up jobs here and there. He worked in gas stations, convenience stores, and in restaurants. Although he was never stable in one job for more than a year, he learned cleaning and cooking while working in these jobs. It is good that he is doing this now."

Maya's response did not indicate ethnicity as a contributing factor to the egalitarian gender relations in her household. Rather, as for Rama and Kanti, changes in the gender of the income earner also altered gendered expectations for reproductive labor at home. When wives became full-time paid workers, they were required to spend long hours on income-generating activities outside their homes, so they did not have time to perform household tasks. In this context, their husbands were compelled to participate in household and reproductive tasks.

Rita, a thirty-eight-year-old housecleaner, lived in New York with her husband and son. She preferred housecleaning jobs to childcare because they gave her more flexibility. She chose her working hours according to her son's school schedule. Rita cleaned about five homes a day, beginning shortly after dropping her son off at school and continuing until her son's school day ended. Back in Nepal, she used to help in her family's garment business, which required her to work outside the home, and she was also responsible for the household tasks. When she came home from work, she cooked, cleaned, and took care of other household matters. Rita's husband rarely participated in household tasks, including taking care of their son and his school-related activities.

Their move to the United States required her husband to participate in the household chores. In Nepal, although Rita worked outside the home, she never received an income or salary. In the United States, her work was more stable than her husband's and she brought in more income. In their home, Rita and her husband shared the household work.[5] When I asked Rita what factors contributed to this shift in the dynamics of their household, she shared:

> Most of the husbands in Nepal don't usually do any household work. They don't cook and clean, there is no such culture. The wives, mothers, sisters, or daughters do the household work. In addition, in the middle-class families, there are helpers and maids. But in America, our situation is different. In Nepal, we had helpers but here I have become one of them. I also leave home early in the morning; he usually works at night. So during the daytime when he is at home, he does the food shopping and cooking. Sometimes if I am working late he brings our son home. Everyone in America does housework, so he also does it. Our American lifestyle taught him this.[6] He now knows that there is no embarrassment in doing housework or helping his wife. He learned how to cook and clean by observation. Now he volunteers to cook even on weekends. Yes, initially he did not have a choice, but now he has become interested in cooking.

5. Rita still did most of the unpaid family work related to her son's personal and educational activities. She scheduled her paid labor according to her son's school and extracurricular activities to better support him.

6. "American lifestyle" refers to their postimmigration household gendered dynamics.

Similar to other participants, Rita indicated that migration changes transnational families' work opportunities and experiences, which in turn changes family lives and the gendered distribution of reproductive work. This was not true for all the women, however. Whereas some husbands were willing to adjust to these postmigration changes, others were reluctant to do so. Some even returned to Nepal. Nonetheless, the move to the United States reframed traditional gender dynamics for some husbands and subverted them for others.

Previous studies have documented changes in the household division of labor and gender relations related to migrant women's engagement in income-generating activities. In her study of Mexican maquiladoras, Fernandez-Kelly (1983) found that gender relations among husbands and wives shifted when women joined the labor force. When women became the sole breadwinners, men performed the household chores and relied on their wives' income. Likewise, Pessar (1999) demonstrates that migrant women actively challenge patriarchal family structures.

Scholars have also analyzed family and gender dynamics precisely through a transnational lens. In their studies of migrant women, Gamburd (2008) and Zontini (2004) discuss the complexities and paradoxes of women's role as breadwinner transnational wives in their personal and married lives. Referring to Filipina domestic workers in Barcelona, Zontini points to contradictions, arguing that women's "earning capacity gives women new control and independence, but also new dilemmas" (2004, 1133), as long-distance conjugal relationships can also strain or dissolve a marriage. Economic autonomy can personally empower women; it can also liberate them from unhappy married life.

Carrasco (2010) also notes that among Peruvian migrants in Chile, women experienced increased personal freedom and conjugal conflict. As she puts it, "Break-ups and contradictions in love relationships are entrenched within the dynamics of the current migration from Peru, as well as in the productive role women have taken, often with increased personal freedom." Moreover, "Cross border migration has further accentuated contradictions between gender ideals and reality, and this is often manifested in partner relationships" (196).

Gendered Culture and Labor: Supporting
and Subverting Patriarchy Simultaneously

Whereas some women and their husbands subverted the traditional gender division of labor, others experienced more contradictory patterns. Naina was a forty-four-year-old New York-based domestic worker doing housecleaning and childcare. During our discussion of shifting gender relations in the family, Naina offered this perspective: "Nepali men look for office work; they don't like to do manual work at all. The other thing is that Nepali wives generally don't want their husbands to struggle in this kind of work so they take on most of the burden. While the Nepali husbands are seeking office work or other nonmanual work, the wives are the ones who bring in the income. This is a growing trend. The gender roles have somewhat switched. The males are home cooking food and looking after the children while the wives are working and making money."

Naina's perspective clearly indicates the ramifications of traditional gendered culture and labor on the Nepali migrant family. Naina lost her husband two years before the study after he died from a stroke. He had never held a steady job in the United States, but occasionally worked here and there. When asked why, Naina replied: "He could not work hard and struggle. I did not mind working and supporting him. Although he didn't have any major health issues at that time, I was concerned and worried about his health. I never asked him to work. He was not very happy with the lifestyle here, I think he was depressed. He wanted to go back to Nepal; we were thinking to go back to Nepal."

Naina's personal story indicates the ramifications of traditional gender ideologies for women and their husbands as they navigated new family and work arrangements in the United States. In Nepal, husbands' occupational status and positions tend to be higher than their wives'. Men are the breadwinners of the family and their socioeconomic status defines the status of the family. Among middle- and upper-middle-class families in particular, husbands are not expected to be involved in household work, and boys are not usually assigned these tasks. When the participants' husbands lost their breadwinner roles and were compelled to participate in so-called women's work (service, domestic), many experienced displacement of their identities. These changes seemed to affect some husbands' mental and physical well-being.

In "Depression in Nepalese Women: Tradition, Changing Roles, and Public Health Policy," Jack and Ommeren (2007) report the ways patriarchy, gender inequality, and a culture of women's oppression contribute to depression in Nepalese women. This study reveals the opposite trend: when gendered household dynamics are reversed in the transnational context, men are subject to depression. It was difficult for these men to cope with work that required obedience and subservience. As one New York-based childcare provider commented, "Men are not used to taking orders, they are used to giving orders. . . . They don't sustain in a job where servitude is expected."

This modification led to some unexpected ramifications. Some husbands preferred to give up their breadwinner roles rather than continue to work in lower-status manual jobs, some preferred to go back to Nepal, some faced health consequences, some did not mind taking on household tasks in their homes.

Jack and Ommeren state: "Women, as a group, place a higher degree of importance on the quality of their personal relationships, and the quality of such relationships centrally affects women's sense of self, self-esteem, and self-regard" (2007, 247). This seemed to be applicable to participants who grew up in more traditional Hindu families. Although the women did not seem to care about the nature and status of their own work and workloads, some indicated that an office job would be better for their husbands' well-being. On a personal level, many participants found income-generating informal work personally liberating; it took them away from their culturally expected roles of subservience and enhanced their familial position and status. Nonetheless, some seemed to be more concerned about their husbands' work status and physical and emotional health than their own. By supporting and confirming their husbands' status in the public arena and not asserting and demanding a consistent income from them, some women also enacted traditional gender ideologies.

During the interviews, some research participants from Brahmin and Chettri ethnic backgrounds indicated their observance of religious fasts and celebration of the Teej festival.[7] These women also adhered to the symbols of their marital status by wearing pote (necklaces made of beads) and red bangles. In one of the focus group interviews, a participant brought red bangles to give to the other married women. Traditionally, a married Hindu woman is supposed to wear a red bangle and pote until she becomes a widow. In a traditional Hindu family, "before marriage, a woman undergoes many *bartas* (religious fasts) in the hope of getting a good husband. After marriage, she undergoes as many *bartas* for her husband's longevity, prosperity, and good health" (Hamal Gurung 2008, 201). The Teej festival, for example, is particularly celebrated among the Hindus; the majority of the Brahmin and Chettri ethnic groups practice Hinduism as both religion and culture.[8]

Although not all the women from Brahmin and Chettri backgrounds adhered to traditional gendered values, the majority of the participants who indicated such gender ideologies were from these ethnic groups. Some from these two groups said that they would have liked their husbands to have higher-status office jobs. When this did not happen, they supported their husbands' desire to quit lower-status jobs or even go back to Nepal.

Paradoxes of Shifting Gender and Power Relations

As I discussed in earlier sections, the effects of women's transnational work in their personal, work, and familial lives have been contradictory (Pessar 1999; Zotini 2004; Alicea 1997; Parreñas 2005; Hamal Gurung 2010; Pessar 2005). Feminist scholars have warned us not to idealize the immigrant family as a coherent social unit with unified family experiences;

---

7. The symbolic value of many Hindu women's religious and cultural fasts, including the Teej festival, center around their husbands' prosperity and longevity. Men do not undergo similar fasting for their wives. The Teej festival started among Hindus. It has become more a gendered cultural event and reflects women's agency. It is also a celebration of womanhood and sisterhood.

8. Religion is a way of life for many Nepalis. Hinduism in that sense implies more than religious identity, it integrates various elements of culture.

doing so may mask the internal conflicts and different interests (Menjivar 2000). Scholars have documented how gender relations are reinvented, renegotiated, and transformed among and within migrant families (Kibria 1994; Pessar 1999; George 2005; Parreñas 2005; Gamburd 2008; Hamal Gurung and Purkayastha 2013).

The women's narratives in this book illustrate the contradictions that emerged when husbands and wives renegotiated gender relations in the family after migrating to the United States. When their wives became the primary paid workers outside the home, some husbands engaged in non-paid household work. This shift destabilized the traditional patriarchal family. However, the arrangement in which women were the primary breadwinners working in the informal domestic and service sectors often came about because research participants and their husbands supported the notion that men should hold higher-status jobs than their wives.

In her ethnographic work *When Women Come First: Gender and Class in Transnational Migration*, George (2005) discusses similar dynamics and tensions among the Keralite immigrant community. She reports that when nurse wives from Kerala first immigrated to the United States and became the main breadwinners for their families, husbands and wives encountered tensions and societal pressure to conform to traditional gendered expectations in the family and community. She reports that the husbands experienced "a loss of status not only at home but also at work and—as marginalized minority men—in the wider society" (13). George's mother was the main breadwinner of the family and her father enjoyed cooking. Nonetheless, at times they conformed to traditional expectations regarding the gendering of household work: "There were times when my mother made a point of cooking when we were expecting company, so that my father would not be teased" (3).

In her study of an immigrant Vietnamese community, Kibria (1994) also notes that a shift in the traditional gendered contributions for husbands and wives creates tensions in the conjugal relationship after immigration. According to Kibria, the "legitimacy of male authority had rested heavily on the ability of men to ensure a middle-class status and standards of living for their families" (253). She argues that because of "the high rate of the men's unemployment, settlement in the United States . . . generated some shifts in power in favor of the women" (252). Such changes enabled women to "construct and channel familial and ethnic resources in ways that they choose" (254). Pessar (1999) also notes that migration simultaneously challenges and reinforces patriarchy in different domains of migrant women and men's lives. The shift in gender relations between Nepali women and their husbands created striking, unique paradoxes. As transnational workers, mothers, and wives, women experienced transformations in their social and economic status. These changes generated contradictory effects in different domains of women's lives. Women faced exploitation in the workplace but empowerment on personal levels. Similar to Kibria's study, as family breadwinners, the participants in this book had the personal autonomy to allocate economic resources as they saw fit. They were also in charge of constructing familial and community arrangements. Meena related her breadwinner role to her enhanced socioeconomic position and personal autonomy: "My economic role has provided me with so many options. I have absolute autonomy in resource allocation and distribution on both familial and community levels . . . I don't have to ask for money from either my son or my husband. I have certainly gained that freedom. We discuss our household, familial, and social issues but I make the decisions. I also make decisions about our Nepal trips—when and for how long. If our relatives or friends want to visit America, my husband leaves it up to me to make a decision about their visit and sponsorship. . . . I see myself as the main decision maker in our household."

Abha was also the main income earner for her family. Her income was crucial for her sons' education and for her family's household expenses, debts, and support of religious institutions in Nepal. Abha's economic contributions to her family and community provided her with a newfound sense of personal efficacy: "I am happy to support my family. Living and working in America has increased my confidence. Now, I feel that I can go anywhere in the world and work. I am no longer dependent on anyone. Rather, I have become the central figure of my family. I make most of the major decisions, especially when it involves money. I have also gained respect from my family and community."

Women's new economic roles, earnings, and income have become vital in their transnational practices. In the next chapter, I discuss women's agency and activism in their social, cultural, and economic transnational practices, and how these engagements and activities have broadened women's sense of accomplishment and empowerment in both local and global contexts.

Conclusion

Nepali women's movement to and subsequent work in the United States added multiple dimensions to their work lives, personal lives, and familial lives. When women became transitional workers, they also became transnational mothers and wives. These multiple roles and identities required changes and sacrifices in familial and conjugal arrangements. As women's narratives indicate, transnational mothers and their children suffered from the spatial separation. However, transnational mothers were constantly engaged and invested in cross-border and long-distance mothering.

The narratives in this chapter also clearly illustrate that Nepali immigrant/migrant women made important economic and social contributions to their families and households on both local and international levels. As the women became the main earners for their families, a shift occurred in their traditional household gender relations. Their voices demonstrate that they were more open to work in the informal service and domestic sectors than their husbands, even though this work involved a loss of status from their work in Nepal. These differences in work patterns between men and women demonstrate the contradictory implications of traditional gender ideologies for migrant/immigrant spouses who must adapt to a feminized global job market. Whereas the research participants were committed to their informal economic income-generating service and care work, their husbands had a difficult time sustaining such jobs.

The narratives also clearly reflect that women and men experienced immigration differently. Gender ideologies informed their responses to household and familial changes postmigration. Whereas women recognized and adapted to the structural constraints imposed by immigration policies in the United States, their husbands were less successful in accepting these changes.[9]

What is striking about women's narratives in this chapter is how traditional gender ideologies caused a *reversal* in the gendered contributions of spouses. Husbands did not want to work in the informal service and domestic sectors because they viewed this work as women's work and as beneath their status as professional men in Nepal. Their inability to work in such occupations led wives to become the family breadwinners, and many husbands even responded to this change by taking on the unpaid reproductive labor at home. These couples thus simultaneously supported and subverted patriarchal ideologies about men and women's contributions to the family.

Thus to comprehend the conditions under which women become transnational workers requires a thorough understanding of women's social, cultural, and economic locations as well as their positions in their families and communities on both local and international levels. It is obvious that women's transnational work and income have multidimensional effects on their lives. These include an economic compulsion to work and support the family combined with economic autonomy and empowerment. Women's contradictory experiences and situations cannot be solely explained within the standard frameworks of the globalization and feminization of informal and service work.

9. During the socialization process, girls are taught to expect and adapt to gender- and familial-based changes. Since Nepal is a patrilocal society, after marriage daughters are expected to live with the husband's or husbands' family. Daughters are considered to be persons who are given away through marriage. So prior to their marriage, girls are taught to adapt to and endure new gender and familial roles in their new families. Since girls are prepared for changes and they move from one family to another, they are more flexible and adaptive to such changes. The younger generation, particularly the educated and professional group, may not hold such gender ideologies, but their parents may still consider or perceive their daughters as persons to be given away.

6

o　o　o

Transnational Community Building

Ties, Connections, and Practices

We plan and organize our sociocultural religious events. . . . We try to
actively participate in our religious celebrations. . . . We also collect donations to support social organizations and deprived community.
　　　　　　　　　　　　　—Childcare provider in New York City

IN THIS CHAPTER, I examine women's agency in building transnational
communities: how their transnational engagement and practices shaped
their lives in the personal, public, and international domains. Specifically,
I am interested in the motivation and rationale for their transnational
activity. Why would women want to send a large portion of their hard-
earned income back home to their family, community, and social organizations? Why devote their precious time outside of work to transnational
or diasporic organizations? After exploring these motivations, I then turn
to the effects of women's activities and financial support. How did family members, community members, and social organizations benefit from
this transnational engagement? And how did it affect the multiple arenas
of women's lives?

Feminist scholars, particularly Chowdhury (2011), Jafar (2011), Moghadam (2005, 2007), Desai (2002, 2009), and Katuna (2012) have documented
South Asian women's transnational organizing and practices. Most of
these studies analyze women's agency and activism at the grassroots
level with NGOs and International NGOs (INGOs). Here I focus on how
a sociopolitically marginalized group of women in the United States

enacted agency and initiated transnational practices that benefitted both local and transnational communities.

I analyze four ways in which the women were engaged in building transnational community: (a) remittances and financial support to family and nonfamily, community, and social organizations; (b) active engagement in building a Nepali diaspora through cultural and social events in America; (c) participation in US-based Nepali nonprofit organizations; and (d) leadership, social networks, and activism.

Transnationalism and Transnational Practices

Being away from their homeland for many years did not diminish the Nepali women participant's sense of connectedness to their families, communities, or nation of origin, or their sense of national identity. Since their migration, these women found new ways of building and maintaining their relationships with local and transnational communities. They were strongly connected to families, communities, and social organizations back home, maintaining these ties through social, political, and economic engagement. Their economic contributions included remittances and gifts sent to immediate and extended family and nonfamily members as well as donations to organizations and institutions. On the surface, these contributions may appear as purely economic, but they also enabled women's engagement in social, cultural, and political transnationalism.

Another way women engaged in transnational practices was by organizing and participating in Nepali social, cultural, and religious events and forums in the United States. Through these events, they kept their home cultures alive and built a strong Nepali diasporic community. These women were also very engaged in local-level fund-raising initiatives and events to support community causes in Nepal.

Most previous studies on gendered labor in a transnational context have focused on women's contributions to the family, such as sending money to support children, spouses, or elderly parents; general contributions to family finances; and building or enlarging family homes (George 2005; Hondagneu-Sotelo 2007; Anderson 2006; Hamal Gurung and Purkayastha 2013). Abbrego found that compared with men migrants, mothers were the most reliable remitters and "invariably remit higher percentages of their earnings and more consistently than fathers" (2009, 1082).

Many participants in this book indeed sent money to their families, including children, husbands, parents, and siblings. They also used their US earnings to buy property in Nepal, land and houses, similar to the Dominican migrant community observed by Levitt (2001) or the Filipino transnational mothers discussed by Parreñas (2005). In addition, however, the women sent money to nonfamily members, social organizations, and NGOs. Another important dimension of their transnational practices was community-based fund-raising in the United States. Katuna's study (2012) on the Nepali Women's Global Network (NWGN), an organization based in the United States, depicts the centrality of women's agency in addressing and making visible Nepali human rights issues in a transnational context. Like the women in Katuna's study, the migrant women in this book did not necessarily use a discourse of human rights to describe their work, but their initiatives and conduct were very much in accordance with a human rights framework.

Women's Civic Engagement and Making a Transnational Community between Family and Community: Transnational Practices

Women in this book participated in various types of transnational activity: they used both formal and informal channels to make economic contributions to communities in Nepal, and they used social and political practices to engage in diasporic community building at both the local and international levels. The contrast between these women's low-paid, low-status work in the informal domestic and service sectors in the United States and their significant economic and personal contributions to Nepal reveal the contradictory relationship between global gendered labor and gendered transnationalism. Most of the women participants lived in the United States alone, without any family. These women allocated approximately 90 percent of their income to their transnational families, communities, and social organizations. This money was remitted in the form of cash gifts, property investments, and donations or community giving. Though women with family in the United States remitted a lower percentage of their income, almost all of the participants sent money to family members, NGOs, schools, or other social organizations. In most cases, remittances were allocated to more than one domain, so that women sent money to social organizations or schools in addition to family members. Although most participants reported that they regularly sent money back home, a few indicated that they did so only periodically.

Syama, whose husband and children lived in Nepal while she lived and worked as a nanny in the United States, sent most of her income to her family and community in Nepal. She also supported a community health center. She described her allocation of income in the following manner:

> SYAMA: My income is $2,000–2,400 a month. If I work overtime, then I make more. For myself, I keep around $400–500; the rest I send to my immediate family members—my husband, daughter, and mother. I also send money to a community health clinic.
>
> SHOBHA: Do you always send money to these family members? Who gets the largest sum of your income?
>
> SYAMA: I always send money to my husband because we are building our own house. So a large portion of my income goes to him. My daughter comes second; she is married and has a son. Currently, she is not working. I try to send her money regularly. Then comes my mother, who suffers from old-age-related health issues. She lives with her sister; my father passed away a long time back. I don't send her money regularly like my husband and daughter, but I send her money at least a few times a year.
>
> SHOBHA: How about the community health clinic? How often do you send them money?
>
> SYAMA: Initially, I was not able to send money to the community health clinic. Now I send money quite regularly. If for some reason I skipped a few months, then I send them money in a lump sum amount.
>
> SHOBHA: You work so hard six days a week. You barely keep any money for yourself. I can understand why you want to invest in family property and why you want to support your family members. But please tell me more about your motivation for supporting the community health clinic.
>
> SYAMA: It's purely for service and helping reasons. . . . My main goal in becoming a nurse was to provide service to needy people and the community.

In Nepal for more than twenty years I provided my services to the people and the poor community in various capacities. As a nurse, I helped them in a hospital. As a social worker and also as a nurse, I provided my services to my neighbors and community. I volunteered at the community health clinic that provided free service for poor people. Then I came here. . . . Since I can't be physically there and provide my services to the people there, I feel more need to support this clinic in whatever capacity I can. I would like to see a continuation of this clinic, because its services have become even more important to the local community. Everything has become so expensive in Nepal; many people struggle for their day-to-day survival. Having access to health care service is a luxury for many of these people. This is why I financially support this clinic.

For single mothers, most of their income went to their children's social and economic well-being. They nonetheless also supported the Nepali social organizations they were affiliated with before coming to the United States. Tara was a single mother whose two children live in Nepal. Although she bore sole financial responsibility for her children, Tara also allocated funds to support a nonprofit organization in Kathmandu that provides adult literacy classes. Before immigrating to the United States, Tara was actively involved with the organization and taught literacy to adult women. Through phone calls and regular remittances, Tara kept her transnational ties alive within and outside her family.

Life was not easy for Tara in the United States, and she worked very hard to earn an income. Yet she sent most of that income home, where it was shared between the family and the social organization. The reason for her remittances to her children is readily apparent. But I was curious as to why she wanted to share her hard-earned income with the nonprofit organization. Tara explained:

I want to support the organization because it's a nonprofit organization. The organization is run by donation and charity. Most of the teachers are volunteers; they don't get any income. The literacy program is for those adults who do not have access to formal education or ways to become literate. I have seen how important it is to learn at least the basic alphabet and basic reading skills. There are many cases in which illiterate people are being deceived. Their family members, relatives, and neighbors unethically take hold of many property-related (land, house) papers that provide consent to these people to be in charge of the property. The illiterate people totally trust them. Since they cannot read, they provide their fingerprints without knowing what's being written. So I would really like to help these people to become literate. The organization provides each of them a notebook and a pen. I know I need to work hard to support the organization, and this issue is so close to my heart. My children are my responsibility, but so is this organization. This organization is for underprivileged people and the community; it is making a difference in many lives. This is a driving force for me to financially support the organization.

Tara's economic transnational practices were rooted in both her mothering and her civic responsibility.

Abha also practiced social, cultural, political, and economic transnationalism. She initially came to the United States to attend an NGO forum in New York. In Nepal, she worked in an NGO and was politically and socially active in her community. She was the chair of her municipality, defeating nine men to win the election. She subsequently became a board member of a Nepali NGO and a lifetime member of the Women's Federation for World Peace. Although she now lived and worked in New York, Abha maintained her connections to the organization. She stated: "I keep in touch with them. Some of my friends who are here in New York wanted to work in the NGO's satellite office here, so I noted their names and sent their names back to my head office in Nepal. The head office in Nepal contacted the office here, so my friends could work in the NGO as well." In this way, Abha bridged the local and transnational, connecting Nepalis in the United States to a broader network of people and activities through the NGO.

Transnationalism helped migrant women deal with the "downward mobility" they experience in the informal service and domestic industries. Through their transnational connections, they found a personal escape from the drudgery and degradation of work in low-status occupations with often exploitative conditions.

Transnational Practices: Beyond Family and Community

Women's remittances and financial support were not limited to family members or to organizations with which they were personally affiliated prior to coming to the United States. Some of the women participants had adult children and did not have an obligation to work and send money back home. Nonetheless, these women worked to financially support nonfamily members and social organizations. In particular, they were invested in the welfare and education of poor children.

Priya had no financial obligations to family members back home. Her only daughter had graduated college and had a good job in Boston. Initially, Priya came to Boston to attend her daughter's graduation, but because of the political situation in Nepal and personal issues, she ended up staying in the United States. Priya did not need to worry about making a living because her daughter supported her financially. Her daughter told her to enjoy life and not to worry about money. But Priya still worked as a childcare provider to financially support two orphan children in Nepal:

> My daughter tells me I don't need to work. She says she will take care of all my needs, and she is doing it. . . . She bought this house, she pays all the bills, she buys food, she even tries to give me pocket money. She wants me to enjoy life and just relax. But I wanted to work and help poor and orphaned children back home. I am supporting two children who live in an orphanage in Kathmandu. They are like my own children. I can't ask my daughter to provide money for these children. I need to work for them. I send money for their education, clothes, and other needs. There are so many orphaned and street children in Nepal. I wish that I could sponsor many of them. If I earn more, then perhaps I can support more children in the future. For this reason, I am working. . . . I don't need to work for my own well-being, but I must work for those children whose future depends on my economic support and care.

In addition to the orphanage, Priya also sent money to a religious organization in North India that provided shelter and education for disabled children. Priya was one of only a few research participants whose transnational giving extended beyond Nepal. When asked, "Why India?"

she replied, "These are needy people. I am supporting the organization for a good cause. Place does not matter. If I had money, I would also like to help needy people here in America. I see many homeless people here and there, and I give them money whenever I can." Priya thus practiced transnational giving in both local and global contexts; she maintained ties with people, communities, and organizations in multiple locations and nations.

Priya's story also reflects her embeddedness in transnational social networks that channeled her contributions to the correct recipients. When I asked Priya about the amount, frequency, and method (including the source and medium) of her remittances, she replied: "I send money through my friends and other social networks. People constantly travel between Boston, New York, and Nepal. It's not hard to find a Nepali every other month or so who visits or goes to Nepal. I send a lump sum of money five or six times a year. There is no fixed amount, but usually it is between $300 and $400. But I make sure that the amount covers the educational and living expenses of my sponsored children and supports the organizations in India. I send the money to my close relatives and they allocate the money between my sponsored children in Nepal and social organizations in India."

Neera, a fifty-seven-year-old childcare provider in Boston, was also committed to financially supporting marginalized children's education. She was particularly compelled to support young girls' education. Her daughter was already married and her son had graduated from a college in the United States. Though she no longer supported her own children financially, Neera chose to provide financial support to a young girl in Nepal. She explained her choice this way: "Education is the most important thing in people's lives. I have experienced this in my own life. I earned an MA in economics, and I worked for a long time as part of the professional staff in a bank in Nepal. My education has affected different aspects of my life, even coming to America. Many poor children, especially girls, don't get an opportunity to go to school. So it is even more important to support a female child's education. That's why I am financially supporting this girl, and I will support her education until her MA degree." Neera had personally experienced the empowering benefits of education, which motivated her to contribute to the girl's education.

Kiran, a forty-three-year-old childcare provider, was actively engaged in transnational practices in New York. She was the founder of a middle school in Kathmandu; she collected and generated funds to help establish the school and was still one of its main financial contributors. The school was free to those who could not afford to pay tuition. Kiran lived in New York with her immediate family members but regularly sent money to assist in the school's operation. Kiran's father, who lived in Nepal, supervised the school. She regularly communicated with her father, the principal, and some teachers by phone and e-mail regarding logistics and student affairs.

Kiran's own two children were getting ready for college, yet she regularly sent money to the school back home. Instead of saving for her own children, she was investing in the futures of needy children in Nepal. Kiran justified her allocation of her earnings this way:

> KIRAN: While growing up, I saw many children around my age who wanted to go to school. But they could not go to school either because of the tuition or other expenses such as books, notebooks, pens, and pencils. Some of those children were in my neighborhood; their parents were very poor. Some of the children even worked to support their parents. This inspired me to do something for those who would not otherwise have the opportunity to attend a school. After high school, I started to tutor some of these neighborhood children at my house. During my college years, I taught part time at a public high school. And I provided free tutoring to economically disadvantaged children. But deep down in my heart, I was determined to establish a middle school for these poor children. Finally, it worked out.
>
> SHOBHA: Tell me how did you start? Can you expand on the financial aspects of the school? Who are the major contributors?
>
> KIRAN: My father knew my plan and passion. In fact, he gave me a piece of land to build a school. Before coming to America, I had asked him if I were to send him some money if he would help me to establish a school in the community. He agreed to do so. After a few months in New York, I began to know more Nepalis in the area. Gradually, I became socially active in the Nepali community. I shared my school plan with some of my friends. They supported my idea. I then informally started to raise funds for the school.

Initially I started with my friends, and then I expanded from the circle of my friends to other social networks. This is how I started.

SHOBHA: Do you still approach your friends or others in the Nepali community to collect funds for your school?

KIRAN: Occasionally I tell my close friends to donate some money to the school, and usually they do. But I haven't approached the larger Nepali community since the school was built.

SHOBHA: How has your living far away affected your roles and responsibilities?

KIRAN: In terms of my financial role and responsibility, I can contribute more now. I can raise and generate more money here than in Nepal. But being far away, I cannot be physically there to teach and supervise the students. The financial aspect is more crucial, though. I still send money regularly. Although the school is nonprofit and most of the people who work there are service oriented, we need some money to run the school.

SHOBHA: Earlier you had mentioned that your own children are getting ready to go to college. Do you think that this will affect your financial support to the school?

KIRAN: Well, I don't think so. I will always keep aside a part of my income. My children can apply for loans and funding to go to college here. They have more alternatives. But the children back home don't have such choices. For that reason, I will continue to financially support the school in Nepal. The value of the dollar is higher than the Nepali currency: $1 is equivalent to 75 Nepali rupees. So even my small financial contribution helps to run the school. The school is making a difference in the lives of many children. It is so gratifying. Service for those who need help is my *dharma.* As long as I am alive, I won't stop helping the school. I will eventually go back to Nepal and will work with these children. I can't think of doing any other thing.

Kiran's responses show that her social and economic transnational practices were rooted in her personal experiences and cultural values. Serving or helping those in need were what she perceived as her *dharma.* In Nepal, where religion is central to most Nepalis' social and cultural life, *daan* (giving), *dharma* (moral and religious duty), and *sewa* (service) are at the core of the two major religions—Hinduism and Buddhism. These religious values are often integrated into social and cultural events and festivals, so that religious, cultural, and civic engagement (sharing, giving, and service to the community) are intertwined. These elements are not only celebrated during special religious events but they are also integrated into the everyday lives of many Nepalis, including women workers in the United States.

The participants were Hindu or Buddhist; some indicated both Hinduism and Buddhism as their religious orientation.[1] Their religious values and elements of their culture influenced their personal and public lives. Rita sent money back home for both family and religious events. Although the frequency and amount varied, a portion of the money usually went for religious purposes. During our interview, Rita told me that other Nepali women migrants in the community regularly sent money to social and religious organizations back home. She shared a case: "Women send their income back home for family and for social causes. I see this person who always wears the same clothes every day. She says that she gives all of her income away to a temple and her family back home. She has two children back home whom she financially supports. I take inspiration from her. She sacrifices personal pleasure for the greater good of the community back home."

Rita's comments about this Nepali woman made me want to know more about her own work life, remittance patterns, and transnational ties. So I asked follow-up questions:

SHOBHA: How well do you know her? Can you tell me a little bit about her work life?

RITA: I know her well. We live in the same apartment complex and I see her almost every day. She shares an apartment with two other Nepali women. I know them too. She works seven days a week. Once I asked her why she was working so hard seven days a week. She then told me that she

1. The simultaneous practice of Hinduism and Buddhism is common in Nepal. I discuss this issue in Hamal Gurung 2003 and 2008.

needed to send money for a temple building construction. She also financially supports two children.

SHOBHA: Earlier you stated that she "sacrifices personal pleasure for the greater good of the community back home." How do you know this? Can you expand on it?

RITA: She just works and works. . . . She does not take any day off. She does not do any fun stuff. She does not even like to go to a shopping mall. I haven't seen her buy clothes or anything for herself. She does not go to the movies and other social or cultural events. She doesn't need to work this hard to support her two children back home. Her parents and husband live in Nepal and they can also take care of the children. She is so much committed to this temple construction in her community. She works so hard, she lives at a bare minimum and gives her income away to the family and community back home. No one is forcing her to sacrifice her personal or social life this way, but she is voluntarily doing it.

Donating money for temples or other religious purposes was a regular activity for many participants. During a focus group discussion, several women reported that they periodically sent money back home to temples and for religious rituals and events such as special *pujas* and *bhajan* (worship, prayer, and chants to particular gods and goddesses). Through their financial support, women maintained their cultural and religious ties with their communities at home. In addition, they used these financial gifts to transfer and localize Nepali rituals, customs, and practices in the United States. In this way, they were simultaneously engaged in local and transnational community building.

Women's Agency: Diasporas, Community Building, and Transnationalism

In *God Needs No Passport: Immigrants and the Changing American Religious Landscape* (2007), Peggy Levitt states, "A transnational perspective tries to look at all layers of social life simultaneously and understand how they mutually inform each other. It recognizes that some social processes happen inside nations while many others, though rooted in nations, also cross their boundaries" (22–23). Schiller, Basch, and Blanc-Szanton (1992) also discuss how transnational migration processes contribute to multiple ties beyond the national borders. Analyzing migrants from St. Vincent, Grenada, the Philippines, and Haiti, they suggest that these migrants "construct and reconstitute their simultaneous embeddedness in more than one society" (48).

Applying a transnational analytical framework to Nepali women's economic remittances reveals the multiple layers of their sociocultural lives. The women in this book constantly employed and transcended the sociocultural practices rooted in their home nation. Their agency was powerful not only in keeping alive ties with family, community, and social organizations back home but also in building and maintaining the social, cultural, and economic landscapes of the Nepali community in the United States. Women sent money back home for social, cultural, and economic reasons and were also engaged in producing and preserving Nepali culture, customs, and rituals in the United States, including religious, social, and cultural events such as the Teej festival, Durga Puja, Luxmi Puja, Satya Narayan Puja, Shree Krishna Janma Astami, the rice feeding ceremony of babies, New Year's celebrations, and wedding ceremonies.[2] Women's agency and leadership were apparent as they planned, organized, and conducted these events. Women were in charge of inviting people, delegating tasks, making food lists, gathering goods, and cooking special delicacies.

In my previous article (2008), I discussed the centrality of women's agency in the religious arena in Nepal: "Religion in Nepal survives largely as a result of women practitioners. It is largely women who practice, protect, and propagate the religion. Be it the daily *puja*, visits to the temple, participation in community prayer groups, systematic adherence to rituals and fasts, it is the womenfolk's continual commitment and active involvement that contributes to the overall vitality of religious life within the home and community" (202).

This fact was also apparent in the lives of many women in this book: their religious practices moved beyond national boundaries. These

---

2. The literal meaning of *puja* is "worship." The term comes from Sanskrit.

women were the producers, builders, and preservers of Nepali culture in the United States. They brought with them symbolic and nonsymbolic cultural elements such as values, beliefs, gestures, music, food, songs, costumes, jewelry, and language—all essential for building a Nepali diaspora and community in the United States. Women celebrated these elements of Nepali culture together in festivals and events. In fact, more than half of the participants reported that they took a turn organizing or coordinating community events. Meeta, a fifty-two-year-old participant, shared with me how the Nepali women celebrate the *Teej* festival in New York:

> We celebrate *Teej* with our friends and family members. Usually, we start our *Dahar Khane* [a female gala and feast with particular delicacies, celebrated on the eve of *Teej*] a week earlier and during the weekend. Because the real *Dahar Khane* may not be on the weekend. We rotate *Dahar Khane* each year among our friends or family members. There are between thirty and fifty women and small children who come to *Dahar Khane*. We don't usually invite the men or the husbands. We do potluck, but the host cooks the main food and delicacies. One of us from the group is in charge of calling people and delegating them a potluck item. People start to come around 5 p.m. We gather, we eat, we sing, and we dance. And of course, we wear our red saris and jewelry. We listen and watch the *Teej* songs on the video. It is so much fun. On the real *Teej* day, we fast the whole day and at night we gather in a Hindu temple in Queens and we perform *puja*. Sometimes we sing and dance after the *puja*, particularly if it is during the weekend. Some women keep fasting until the next morning.

When I asked Meeta about the purpose of celebrating *Teej* in the United States, she replied: "This is our culture, we have been doing it for a long time, and we'll continue doing it. It is even more important to celebrate *Teej* here for our community. The younger generation will learn from us."

Hema was also active in organizing and coordinating cultural events in the Greater Boston area. She echoed Meeta's belief in the importance of celebrating Nepali traditions in the United States: "This is to give continuity to our culture. Just by moving to a different land does not mean that we can't live our social and cultural lives here. Building a cultural community is even more important when we live far away from our home and community. Our sociocultural events and celebrations allow us to bring the Nepali community together and teach our children about our sociocultural heritage. This is part of who we are. . . . We try to pass the cultural values onto the new generation, and we hope that they will carry on."

These insights highlight why and how women participated in Nepali cultural events. Their voices clearly reflect the value of these events to the Nepali diaspora and community in the United States. The women perceived these events as part of their Nepali roots and identity, so it was important for them to build and maintain its practices.

The migration process and living in a foreign land also presented some challenges to Nepali women's celebration of cultural events. First of all, owing to the time difference, major festivals could not be observed or celebrated at the exact date and time as in Nepal.[3] Second, in US society, these are not widely observed events for which businesses are closed and workers excused from their duties. Therefore, as Meeta described, these festivals had to be celebrated during weekends. Third, because Nepali people worked in both the formal and informal labor markets, finding a date and time that worked for all community members was challenging. Finally, organizing a cultural program that includes traditional songs and dance and involves cooking traditional foods and delicacies required time, effort, and energy.

Nepali women migrants were agents who transformed social and cultural values and practices in transnational spaces as they collectively built a Nepali identity and cultural community. Women were also adaptive to structural and spatial changes. They modified their practices to give continuity to the Nepali sociocultural landscape in the face of new and different structural conditions. As organizers and sponsors, these women were central to cultural events and to their community. Their active participation extended women's power beyond the household and into the community.

---

3. I address these issues in "Growing Up Hindu: Mapping the Memories of a Nepali Woman in the United States" (2008).

In "Migration and Vietnamese American Women: Remaking Ethnicity," Kibria documents similar trends: "The social networks of the Vietnamese American women were central to the dynamics and organization of the ethnic community. . . . The women's centrality to these social networks gave them the power not only to regulate household exchange but also to act as agents of social control in the community in a more general sense. . . . The relative rise in power that had accrued to the Vietnamese American women as a result of migration expressed itself in their considerable influence over the organization and dynamics of the ethnic community" (1994, 257).

As a Nepali woman migrant in the United States, I have personally witnessed the significance of religious festivals and celebrations to the lives of the migrant Nepali community. In the absence of close family members, immigrant Nepalis rely on ties to a broader diasporic community. Narrating my own cultural experience as a Nepali migrant woman in the United States, I noted: "Migrant women workers have come together through casual social gatherings and celebration of festivals to undertake a wide variety of economic, cultural, and religious tasks. They have established and created social ties that form the basis of many alliances and support networks that extend throughout the community. Similarly, in the United States, being away from home, people and communities have become surrogate kin. . . . As a family of friends, they share both happy and sad moments: life-altering events such as a birth, a wedding, or death" (2008, 206).

Other scholars have also documented the importance of religious and social engagements in the lives of immigrant communities (George 2005; Levitt 2007; Ranjeet 2008; Narayan and Purkayastha 2008). Religious affiliation and participation helped Chinese immigrant women to confront familial, social, and economic challenges during the settlement process in London, Ontario (Da 2010). Similarly, George (2005) notes the importance of the Indian Christian church in the social lives of the Keralite immigrant community in this way: "Without relatives or friends nearby, my family found community and support in the immigrant Indian Christian church. The church service—which took place in rented halls in the early years—met both a religious and a social need for us. . . . Our social lives revolved around the church as church members became our extended family and community in the United States" (3).

Transnationalizing Women's Agency:
From Activism to Global Civic Engagement

Women's transnational practices extended beyond sending remittances and capital investments to their families, communities, and social organizations back home. They extended even beyond women's efforts to build and maintain a Nepali sociocultural landscape in the United States. The participants in this book actively engaged in local and transnational social organizations in the United States to raise funds for social organizations back home. Women's fundraising initiatives were distinctive markers of their global civic engagement.

In the early 1990s, there were only a handful of formally registered Nepali organizations in the United States. Initially, professional Nepalis took the initiative to establish a social organization for social and cultural forums and interactions. But as the Nepali community started to grow in the United States, Nepali social organizations also grew in nature and scope. In the earlier years, social organizations focused on the sociocultural lives of the immigrants and nonimmigrant Nepali communities. Gradually, Nepali social organizations became much broader and transnational. Now, there are many gender, labor, immigration, humanitarian, human rights, and social-justice-oriented Nepali social organizations in the United States. In Boston and New York, Adhikaar for Human Rights & Social Justice, the Greater Boston Nepali Community, the Help Nepal Network, the Himalayan Foundation, and the Nepali Women's Global Networks are all prominent social organizations. The boards and the executive committees of these organizations are primarily composed of professionals and well-established immigrants, but despite their lower professional status and shorter immigration history, the women in this book were enthusiastically and persistently engaged in the organizations. The women came together with others in the Nepali community for a common purpose.

As I discussed in previous chapters, many of the women participants were NGO workers back home. In the United States, these women worked in the informal domestic or service economy; however, this did not stop their participation in NGO work. The women brought their NGO-based aspirations and legacies with them. During the second round of follow-up interviews, ten participants (six from the Boston area and four from New York City) reported that they were involved with fund-raising initiatives in US-based Nepali nonprofit organizations. Two participants even became the elected members of the Greater Boston Nepali Community's advisory board. All of these women helped the organizations they were affiliated with generate resources to help people and communities in Nepal.

Bijaya, a thirty-nine-year-old childcare provider, was one such participant. She was deeply involved with a Nepali nonprofit organization in Boston. She helped the organization raise funds for communities in need in Nepal. Bijaya worked in the informal sector and she had a large social network of friends and acquaintances that also worked in the informal labor market. In her fund-raising initiatives, Bijaya engaged and included these women in particular. She explained:

> Usually, the board members of the organization contact me to help them raise funds. I know lots of people that they might not know. So, I am usually in charge of contacting these people. Initially, I contact my friends and acquaintances through phone calls. I ask them for a meeting and we discuss the date and time that would work for most of them. Generally, we meet on the weekend, especially on Sunday. Once we decide the date and time, we decide the place for our meeting. Usually, we meet in one of our friend's houses; these meetings also serve as our social event. We cook, we eat, and we catch up on lots of other things. During the meeting, we discuss the reasons for and the importance of our donations to the social organizations in Nepal or for Nepalis. We discuss the nature and the quality of the work that the social organizations in Nepal are doing—for whom the money is being sent.

I knew that some research participants had direct personal, social, and economic ties with communities and social organizations in Nepal. I was therefore curious as to whether women contributed to these social organizations through other US-based Nepali social organizations. When

I raised this issue, Bijaya replied, "Yes, they do." Knowing how hard some of the women worked and how little money they made, it seemed unrealistic that they would be able to donate money through multiple channels (personal ties and nonprofit organizations) and to more than one organization. So I asked Bijaya whether there was a fixed amount of money for such a donation and if not, how much money people gave at a time. She replied: "We don't set a fixed amount. It is totally up to them or whatever they can afford to give. But usually people don't say no. There is a wide range of fund-raising events, which welcome any amount of giving. Usually, the donation varies between $10 and $100. We even have a $1 program that many of my friends are involved in. I tell people about these different programs and organizations through which they can help Nepal and Nepalis."

Anita, a fifty-one-year-old childcare provider, was one of Bijaya's friends. She was considered a leader among the women who worked in the service, domestic, and childcare sectors. Anita helped newcomers find jobs and places to live. She took time off from her own job to show these women around the city, explain how the transportation system works, and provide information about basic matters (food, grocery, laundry). Occasionally, she organized and hosted a potluck lunch or dinner where she introduced women to one another. The women looked to Anita for various kinds of personal and professional suggestions and help.

Anita was also well known for her fund-raising. She helped Nepali organizations raise and collect funds for social issues in Nepal. Like Bijaya, she also mobilized women for fund-raising programs. She was instrumental in collecting donations from her circle of friends and acquaintances, which included the majority of participants who resided in the Greater Boston area. I asked her about the kinds of organizations she was involved with and her roles in them. She responded:

ANITA: I am a member of the Greater Boston Nepalese Community organization and I am really involved in that. The organization provides all kinds of help and information to both the immigrant and nonimmigrant Nepali community. It organizes social and cultural events for Nepalis. It also collects money and donations for social issues in Nepal. . . . Recently, each of us donated $50 to a public school back in Nepal. I am also involved in the $1 program; the money we collect primarily goes to needy and poor children back home.

SHOBHA: Do you collect money for any other issues than children's education?

ANITA: Yes! We collected money recently and we still haven't really decided what to do with that money. My friends and I are getting together to discuss this soon.

SHOBHA: So that money collection was a separate initiative then?

ANITA: Yes, some of my friends and I have also started collecting money for marginalized and helpless people like victims of domestic violence, orphans, disabled and ill, widows, elders . . . and we are thinking to donate our money each time to a separate group . . . so that everyone one will get something. . . .

SHOBHA: Tell me what really motivates you and other women to engage in such fund-raising programs and donate money.

ANITA: When you are far away from your home, community, and your country, you love them more. You feel for them when you live so far away. So you want to give, give, and give. This is my personal experience, but many other women feel the same. Now, we know that our small donation can make a difference to many lives in Nepal. For that reason, whenever there is an opportunity to do something like this we don't think twice. This allows us to help our community and do something for our country. Some of our friends are already affiliated with some social organizations back home. So whenever people visit Nepal, we try to send some money to these organizations. Sometimes we don't have enough time to organize a meeting to collect money. In those particular situations, we discuss the issue by phone . . . usually, two people coordinate the phone calls and they visit people's houses and collect donations.

SHOBHA: How long are you planning to continue in such activities? How do you perceive the roles of the Nepali community in organizing and maintaining economic support to Nepal and Nepalis?

ANITA: There is no end of it . . . I will continue supporting community and social organizations here and back home. I know most of my friends will continue to do the same. And there are more and more Nepalis coming to

America these days, and there are more Nepali students graduating from US colleges and universities. I think there will be more Nepali organizations in the United States in coming days, and it is my hope that there will be more fund-raising initiatives and donations for needy people and social organizations. . . . I think this will also help the country in the long run.

Anita's fund-raising activities demanded significant time, energy, and resources from Anita and her friends, all of whom were migrant workers, but they were dedicated to this humanitarian charity work. As Levitt suggests, "When a small group is regularly involved in its sending country, and others participate periodically, their combined efforts add up. Taken together and over time, they are a social force that can transform the economy, values, and everyday lives of entire regions" (2007, 23). This pattern has already emerged among Nepali women migrants. The participants' transnational economic practices made a difference to many lives, communities, and social organizations within and beyond Nepal. Their remittances also contributed to the national economy. In this sense, these women were truly a transformative social force.

The women participants were heavily involved with social organizations and NGOs in Nepal before they migrated. It is likely that this involvement had some influence on their fund-raising work after migrating. It would be interesting to examine whether Nepali migrant women who do not have NGO affiliations exhibit similar patterns.

Activism, Transnationalism, and Empowerment: From Local to Transnational

When women become their families' main income earners, gender relations within families shifted. As a consequence, women experienced increased decision-making power and personal autonomy in their families and in their communities. How did these changes in gender relations affect women's autonomy and decision-making power at the transnational level?

Women conducted their lives in many different domains (personal, work, family, community) and on multiple levels (local, national, transnational); their economic roles were different in each of these contexts.

Although it cannot be said which arena was most affected by the women's new economic roles, the women experienced effects in both their personal and public lives. Their transnational practices made their contributions and leadership visible both locally and transnationally. Women organized together to build, support, and preserve a transnational community. Their agency and activism were apparent in their social, cultural, and economic transnational practices.

One of the contradictions that emerged in several women's stories was their loss of social position and professionalism on their move to the United States. Ironically, the money they earned through low-status, low-paying jobs allowed women to engage in the transnational practices through which they enacted their capabilities and maximized their potential. This money helped them invest in cultural, religious, social, and economic capital and engage in humanitarian projects in a broader context. In turn, women's leadership in these arenas helped them achieve respect and status on familial, societal, national, international, and transnational levels. Here is how one participant described her downgraded work, which also allowed her to make transnational economic contributions:

> I was very proud of the status that I had in Nepal as a teacher and as a social worker. But after coming here, I feel guilty that I am a babysitter. However, I also send money back to the organization that I used to work with, and I feel like I have given back a lot to the organization. I'm going to stay a few years and keep supporting the women's organization back in Nepal. I hope that when I go back, the women will respect me because I was not working for just my personal concerns. In addition, some of the money that I am investing in the joint university goes to help the kids of poor families. The kids can get scholarships to study in the university. I feel like I have contributed to the Nepalese society.

Several research participants reported that their economic contributions and transnational practices had improved their personal and public lives, boosting their self-confidence and self-esteem. Abha was socially and politically active in Nepal. The scope of her activism, however, became much broader and global in the United States. Abha experienced downward job mobility, but the money her jobs generated allowed her to build transnational assets and transnational ties. This boosted her self-confidence. She was proud of being able to support needy people back home. Abha put it this way: "I think my self-respect has been most affected. The job that I hold now solves my economic problems. But when I helped needy people back home, I was proud of myself and my job. Performing this job has made me stronger internally. Yes, this process has definitely made me courageous. If women gather their courage and act accordingly, then they can do anything."

For Anita, women's empowerment came from within. Like Abha, Anita's activism was much broader in scope. She shared her personal experiences in this way:

> Social networks, leadership, collective initiative, and activism are important for us. We can achieve empowerment through women's agencies and activism. If we organize and mobilize our strength and visions, we can accomplish any mission and on any level. But we have to have the passion and interest to work for common goals. In Nepal, I helped only a few women in my community. Now I work with many other women . . . we gather people, we raise funds, and we send money to needy people and social organizations. Working this way and helping others is a rewarding experience. It is a quite uplifting and empowering experience, and it allows us to be leaders, decision makers, and contributors. People recognize and appreciate our initiatives and contributions here and there, in the family and community, and internationally.

Other research participants—Hema, Shyma, Bijaya, and Meena in particular—also recognized the power of women's networks, agency, and activism in transnational initiatives and practices.[4] They indicated a linkage between women's social networks, transnational practices, and increased autonomy and decision-making power. All three reported that

---

4. In my previous research on women carpet weavers (2003), I showed examples of how the women weavers constantly use social networks in their everyday lives.

their economic contributions and transnational engagement on both local and international levels had increased their status and positions beyond their family and community.

Although the majority of the participants' economic support to nonfamily members and social organizations was service oriented and humanitarian in nature, their giving and donations also had social, cultural, economic, and political implications. Women's economic remittances and donation-giving patterns indicated both symbolic and practical relevance. For some, their giving was form of cultural, religious, and spiritual engagement; others used their contributions to build a path that would result in higher status when or if they returned to Nepal.[5]

One interesting fact is that all research participants, even those who immigrated to the United States after winning the DV lottery, indicated that they would eventually return home to Nepal. None of the women had a desire to retire in the United States. Thus, women's economic transnational activities were also used to prepare public and political spaces for their eventual return to Nepal.

Women's Agency and Activism: From Personal to Political

Women's agency and activism were also apparent in the participants' collective efforts to learn about and to achieve their civil and workplace rights.[6] During the second phase of my interviews in 2009, the state government of New York was discussing a law to grant workplace rights to domestic workers. This issue was very relevant to the lives of the participants. Most of the women, particularly those in New York, were aware of the bill and its ramifications. In fact, some had started to participate in community-based advocacy groups and campaigns for domestic workers' rights. A few women knew about Adhikaar, a New York-based Nepali

5. Women's transnational activism may be partially a calculated move to diffuse and deflect societal and family judgments about their living and working away from family. In this sense, activism can be viewed as a tool to preempt patriarchal questioning and categorizations by family, friends, and community.

6. An in-depth exploration and analysis of workplace rights is vital. Further research should examine these issues.

nonprofit organization that advocates for civil rights, human rights, and social justice.[7] These women had learned about Adhikaar through their social networks and in turn told other women about Adhikaar. When women met at community events or hosted an event at their homes, they shared information about Adhikaar and other relevant organizations. Some of the women were in direct contact with Adhikaar, seeking more information about their civil and workplace rights. When they learned something new, they informed other women through phone calls and e-mails. Women were thus sharing awareness about their rights.

During the interview phase, the status of the bill to grant workplace rights to domestic workers was being discussed, and the women were concerned about its possible ramifications. Since it appeared that the civil and workplace rights of women in this industry would remain restricted, Nepali women mobilized at the personal and the community grassroots levels to discuss alternative methods to obtain their labor rights. Some established informal support groups and networks, which provided a platform to share views and issues. They discussed their problems and identified goals. Together, they approached the director of Adhikaar and found an advocate who would work for their rights. Through their collective efforts, women's agency shifted from personal and household affairs and transnational community building into political spaces and the global discourse on human rights.

Conclusion

In this chapter, I discussed Nepali women's participation in transnational spaces. Through various forms of cultural, social, and economic transnational engagement and practices, women built local and transnational lives and communities. By engaging in everyday Nepali sociocultural practices—such as conducting *puja*, keeping religious fasts, maintaining rituals (particularly those related to life and death), planning

---

7. In the Nepali language, the term *adhikaar* refers to rights. Adhikaar is partnered with Domestic Workers United and the National Domestic Workers Alliance in New York. These organizations work together closely for domestic workers' rights.

and organizing festivals—these women maintained a connection to Nepal that transcended national boundaries and strengthened the diasporic community.

Through economic and sociocultural transnationalism, Nepali women in the United States transformed the lives of people and communities back home. A gendered and racialized expectation exists in the academic literature and in popular culture that low-wage women migrant workers are enmeshed in their families. Nepali women's remittances and donations certainly strengthened their families and their own position within the family but they also extended well beyond their families to support religious, social, and community causes back home. Women acted as family breadwinners, supported extended family, made investment in real estate, supported those in need, and supported social organizations in Nepal financially. Through their contributions these women transformed the social, cultural, and economic landscapes they came from.

Women's new economic roles figured most prominently at the intersection of their personal and transnational experiences. On a private level, women's agency in terms of economic remittances and community-building practices contributed to their self-confidence, self-esteem, decision-making power, and empowerment. On a public level, their remittances and organizational work altered the political and economic landscape of Nepal as a nation.

The Nepali women I interviewed felt a strong sense of responsibility for and commitment to global citizenship and civic engagement. Whether as a care worker in the workplace, a transnational mother away from her children, or a global citizen engaged in service or humanitarian work, these women provided the physical and emotional labor to care for and nurture others locally and transnationally. In this way, women blurred the boundaries between local and global in civic engagement and citizenship. In their article "Care Work: Invisible Civic Engagement," Herd and Meyer write: "We infuse gender into the civic engagement debate by arguing that care work, defined as the daily physical and emotional labor of feeding and nurturing citizens, is an active form of participatory citizenship with far-reaching benefits" (2006, 325).

Employing their leadership skills, women also formed networks that helped them build a diasporic community locally and transnational service and activism globally. These groups provided women a forum to learn and share information about their global engagement, civic responsibilities, workplace rights, and human rights. In this context, women were the agents of transformational social change and their sociocultural, political, and economic activism transcended national and international boundaries.

7

o   o   o

Conclusion

From Informal Workers to Transnational Community Builders

I have been living here for more than a decade . . . I am still doing the same work . . . but I have changed my work many times. Work is just one aspect of my life . . . I am very much involved with the Nepali community and other nonprofit organizations both in the United States and Nepal. I am Nepali wherever I live, and I help the people and community however I can.

—Childcare provider and convenience store worker in Boston

THIS BOOK told the stories of Nepali women who came from professional and semiprofessional backgrounds but migrated to the United States to work in the domestic and service sectors of the informal economy. In each chapter, I focused on a particular aspect of the women's lives. The women's voices provided a rich picture of transnational lives embedded in multiple layers of community. These women exercised their agency as women migrants through various avenues, from seeking personal freedom to engaging in transnational citizenship.

Women's narratives are at the core of this book. In this concluding chapter, I revisit some of these narratives to recount the major trends they revealed. In chapter 2, the participants clearly described some emerging trends in Nepal's migration history. As part of the global "feminization" of migration, these Nepali women initiated family migration or migrated alone, breaking the traditional pattern of men leaving Nepal as the lead migrants. Whereas the literature on feminized migration from the Global

South points to the push/pull factors of a lack of income-earning opportunities in the homeland and the availability of service work in the global
cities, Nepali women's paths to migration were more complicated. In most
cases, these women's migration involved a combination of social, cultural,
political, economic, and transnational factors. The experiences of Gina,
Tara, Priya, and Hema presented in chapter 2 showed that their decisions
to migrate to and work in the United States were both personal and structural. Their social networks and transnational ties mediated their migration process.

Gina's story reflects the intersecting factors that led many participants to migrate to Nepal. Gina came from an upper-middle-class family
in Nepal. She had attended an expensive prep school in India and lived a
privileged life. But when she became a mother without a formal wedding,
she faced scrutiny and humiliation, particularly from the media. Gina's
choice to bear a child without a wedding reflected an emerging trend in
Nepal in which women are beginning to break from traditional expectations regarding gender and family. But by deviating from mainstream
norms, Gina encountered a gendered culture of oppression from social,
religious, legal, and political institutions. Because of this oppression, she
wanted to move away from Nepal. Her class privileges and transnational
social networks facilitated her move to the United States. Had she not had
a family who could finance her trip to the United States with her daughter
and transnational ties in Boston, perhaps she would not have made the
decision.

Syama was a well-established nurse in a top hospital in Kathmandu.
She came from a middle-class family in Kathmandu. She was also a
respected social worker in her community. She came to the United States
because through her professional networks she knew friends in the
United States who were able to help her secure a visa. Her middle-class
status and resources enabled her to pay the visa application fee, airfare,
and other travel-related expenses. Without her networks and income, Syama's choice to migrate would not have been possible. But because of her
own status and her connections to the established Nepali community in
the Boston area, she was able to extend her stay and work in the informal
economy in the United States.

The narratives in this book clearly show that women migrate both for personal reasons and in response to structural changes in Nepal as a sending country and the United States as a receiving country. The growing Nepali community in the United States and the establishment of transnational organizations provided women with a diasporic community to rely on after migrating. This was not the case in the 1980s or even in the early 1990s.

There are many variations in women's migration stories. As I discussed in chapter 2, each woman's case was unique—the determining factors varied from personal to political and from micro to macro. To analyze their migration process only through the phenomenon of globalization would therefore be a gross oversimplification.

The literature on women migrant workers working in the informal economy also tends to focus on one set of demographic and socioeconomic backgrounds,[1] presuming women migrants to be from a lower socioeconomic background, uneducated, and unprofessional. This book challenges such assumptions. Like Gina and Syama, most women participants came from middle-class family backgrounds, had a college-level education, and had held a professional or semiprofessional job back home.

Neither Gina nor Syama came to the United States intending to work in the informal service sectors, but they both ended up doing so. This was also the case for many other women who initially came for a short-term visit with friends or family members or to attend a professional event. So why did these professional women with respectable jobs back home end up staying and working in the informal and service sectors?

The women's move to the United States and their decision to stay and work there indicated some major trends. One is a link between a gendered migration pattern and major shifts in Nepali social, political, and economic landscapes. Others include a culture of gender oppression, providing an incentive for women to emigrate; women's transnational ties brought about by prior international migration and their involvement with

---

1. Popular culture, especially Hollywood films, perpetuates the stereotypes of nannies and domestics as uneducated and unprofessional.

international NGOs; gender, social class, and country-specific migration patterns; and women's agentic transnational practices. Women's migration to the United States followed a civil war in Nepal that fomented a democratic movement and a women's movement in addition to political and economic upheavals.

Nepali women's migration to the United States reflects class- and country-specific migration patterns. Women from lower socioeconomic communities in Nepal tend to seek employment as domestics in Gulf and Southeast Asian nations (Bhadra 2007). The women in this book, however, were from middle-class, professional, and semiprofessional backgrounds and did not initially migrate to work in the domestic sectors, though most of them eventually did so. This suggests that regardless of socioeconomic status or reasons for migration, migrant women tend to be employed in the female-dominated service and domestic sectors.

Between Informal Sector Work and Intersectionality: Exploitation or Empowerment?

This book illustrates some dualities of informal sector work and intersectionality of race, ethnicity, gender, nationality, and citizenship. Chapter 3 showed that women were both attracted to and absorbed into informal economic work. Their narratives revealed the advantages and disadvantages of working in the informal sector.

In terms of work conditions and labor relations, these women's experiences were reminiscent of the work lives of Caribbean, Latina, Central American, and Asian domestic workers. As in other studies (e.g., Rollins 1985; Romero 1992; Chang 2000), women in this book encountered exploitative work conditions. Despite their middle-class and professional backgrounds, the women were not able to escape poor work conditions and abusive labor relations. Their race, nationality, citizenship, and immigration status made them vulnerable in the workplace. Examples in chapter 4 show that women's work lives often involved long days and long nights on the job. For a live-in nanny, it was especially hard to determine when paid work began and ended. Whenever a child was sick or just could not sleep, whenever there were social events at the employers' house, whenever employers had to attend social gatherings outside the home—in all these instances, it was the live-in nanny's responsibility to take care of the kids, without overtime pay or extra time off. In this sense, the women had no control over their labor.

On a personal level, the women resisted exploitative labor conditions. When their work became unbearable, women would quit their jobs. Individual actions, however, did not liberate women from abusive labor conditions in the long run. When they took another job, they often encountered similar labor relations.

What seemed to be the most dehumanizing work experience was the accusation of stealing. When Maya and Kabita were accused of stealing, they felt that their dignity had been violated. The emotional trauma they suffered was similar to the psychological exploitation women domestics documented in Judith Rollins's book *Between Women: Domestics and Their Employers* (1985). Rollins discusses how different forms of exploitation in domestic service are tied in with the employer-employee relationship. As she poignantly puts it, "What makes domestic service as an occupation more profoundly exploitative than other comparable occupations grows out of the precise element that makes it unique: the personal relationships between employers and employee. What might appear to be the basis of a more humane, less alienating work arrangement allows for a level of psychological exploitation unknown in other occupations. The typical employer extracts more than labor" (156).

Like many Latina immigrants (Hondagneu-Sotelo 2007), Nepali women were expected to perform tasks unrelated to the position for which they were hired. This was apparent in many narratives. Women's employers made or changed work policies at any time, expecting the women to perform additional household tasks such as cooking and cleaning, demanding extra hours of work without raising wages, and changing work schedules without consulting the women. The women's work, however, had many dimensions. The exploitative work conditions and abusive labor relations was just one set of realities. Nepali women worked in a market that was segmented not just by race and gender but also by pan-ethnicity and the South Asian diaspora. Cross-Atlantic regional relationships were apparent in hiring practices and in all kinds of employment in the informal economy, including care work, restaurant work, convenience store work, and so on. Nepali women and their Indian employers sought each other out for their shared culture, language, food, and religion. Abha and Meena's stories typified this trend.

The commonalities between employers and employees engaged in pan-coethnic relations as members of the South Asian diaspora did not liberate women from exploitative labor conditions. In fact, these sociocultural relations often blurred the boundary between paid and unpaid work when a woman worker became "like family," intensifying her workload. This was the case for Abha, whose employers gave her a handbag on Mother's Day to symbolize her position in the family. She also excitedly told me that her employers, like her, were devotees of the goddess Durga. But at the same time, her employers expected her to cook food for the family and trained her to work in their health clinic during the weekend. Abha's situation was thus contradictory and her feelings ambivalent.

This bears repeating: the relationship between women workers and their pan-coethnic Indian employers presented two extremes—familiarity and intimacy on a cultural level and unequal labor relations on an employment level. These extremes often generated complex and polarized labor relations.

Gender Roles and Gender Relations: Localizing and Transnationalizing

By moving or migrating to the United States and by being the most significant economic contributors to their families and local and transnational communities, the women in this book simultaneously deconstructed traditional gender relations and reconstructed new ones. In the process of adopting and internalizing new gender roles in the private and public domains, some women and their husbands simultaneously supported and subverted traditional roles.

The patriarchal gender socialization of Nepali women and men and their newly acquired gender roles and relations in the United States generated interesting gender shifts and paradoxes. The paradoxes lie in the interplay between patriarchy and women's transnational work. Whereas the majority of the women had the desired personal qualities (adaptive, accommodating, flexible, compassionate, patient, multitasking) to cope with informal work life in the United States, men lacked such qualities. The very qualities that made Nepali women an ideal workforce also enabled them to embrace a new way of thinking about their relations with men and the broader society.

In my previous work on women in carpet production in Nepal (2003), I analyzed the contexts in which class, caste, ethnicity, gender, and paid work had the greatest impact on the status, authority, and relative autonomy of women in the carpet manufacturing sectors of Nepal. One of the significant findings of that study was the correlation between paid work and women's enhanced household decision-making power. Women's narratives in this book indicated a similar trend but on a much broader scale—indeed, on a transnational level.

Transnationalizing Women's Agency, Activism, and Humanitarian Citizenship

Although confined to degrading informal sector work, exploitative work conditions, and abusive and humiliating labor relations, women found a way to disengage from such work situations and to rise above it. Narratives throughout the book demonstrated the power of women's agency through transnational economy contributions and diasporic community building. Women persistently acted on their agency to build and rebuild the Nepali community in the United States, organize community events, mobilize groups for fund-raising events, pull together resources to help their communities and socially and economically marginalized people, and organize themselves. These paths helped women rise above exploitative work conditions and abusive labor relations.

Women allocated their hard-earned income in different directions and to different groups (family members, the community, social organizations); through these remittances and donations, they actively participated in social, cultural, and economic transnationalism. Their voices affirmed their passion to help socially and economically marginalized and deprived communities. The majority of the women were engaged in some form of philanthropic work through which they experienced personal fulfillment. The women's economic support of their family and social organizations enhanced their position and status in the household and on an international scale. Through their social, cultural, political, and economic transnational practices and their own agency, they experienced contentment and empowerment. Women's agency and collective efforts enabled them to overcome structural challenges and regain the respect lost through their declining professional status. This reaffirms both the feminist and sociological importance of human agency and collective action for social and global change.

Informal Workplace and Nongovernmental Organizations: Transnationlizing Human Rights and Global Work Policies

When I began this book in 2005, domestic workers along with NGO and INGO communities had started a movement for domestic workers' rights in New York. The housekeepers, childcare providers, and elderly caregivers had united and collectively called for action. In 2009, when I was conducting follow-up interviews with women, New York State was about to pass the Domestic Workers Bill. In 2010, when I was starting to analyze women's narratives, the state finally passed the Domestic Workers Bill of Rights and became the first state to take such a step. Were there any ramifications from these initiatives Nepali women working in New York City?

Women in this book were not directly involved with the domestic rights movement in New York City, but some of the participants were in contact with the Nepali New York-based nonprofit organization Adhikaar. Adhikaar deals with social justice and human rights issues and partners with Domestic Workers United and the National Domestic Workers Alliance in New York. During the period of researching and writing this book, some women in the New York area were actively gathering and sharing information regarding domestic workers' rights through Adhikaar. Some women workers in the Boston area had also heard about Adhikaar and were planning to contact the organization. The community-based outreach events of both Nepali and non-Nepali nonprofit workers' organizations in the United States generated awareness about civil and domestic workers' rights among Nepali women. At the time, women still had no control over their labor and labor conditions. This book therefore calls for action and lays the groundwork for women's labor and human rights.

As discussed earlier, women's agency was powerful in building and rebuilding their transnational community in the United States and Nepal. Although the women themselves were a vulnerable and marginalized workforce in the United States, that did not stop them from mobilizing and allocating resources for marginalized communities back home. Nepali women were actively engaged in nonprofit organizations (including Help Nepal, GBNC, and Walk for Nepal, among others) in both the United States and Nepal. However, women's networks rarely extended beyond the Nepali diaspora. In the future, I hope to see Nepali women expand their circle of international community and transnational networks. By joining forces with local, national, and international organizations and communities, these women would be in a better position to advocate for their civil, labor, and human rights. Affiliating with various grassroots, national, and international organizations that work specifically on labor and human rights issues will provide women with avenues and platforms to voice their labor concerns, learn about workers' rights, and mobilize for justice.

Community-based grassroots organizations such as the Brazilian Women's Group in Boston and Domestic Workers United in New York have already illustrated the power of domestic workers' social and political initiatives and activism. There is also a trend among US-based Nepali organizations to integrate the human rights conversation into their other concerns. The Nepali Women's Global Network (NWGN) is one such organization. Although NWGN does not necessarily use a discourse of human rights, the organization is doing human rights work (Katuna 2012). NWGN addresses the civil and human rights issues of the Nepali community.

Women had limited options to demand their workplace rights. With the help of relevant organizations and by employing their own agency, women can mobilize activism for social and workplace justice. The feminist scholars Valentine M. Moghadam (2005, 2007), Manisha Desai (2009), and Elora Halim Chowdhury (2010) have already documented women's vital initiatives to transnationalize activism. These scholars illustrated the potential of women's agency and transnational activism to create a just society.

Broader Impacts and Relevance of This Book

Through various examples, I offered readers insights into the lived experiences of Nepali migrant women and connect those insights to the broader issues of gendered labor, transnationalism, and women's agency and empowerment. These Nepali women lived in the context of a changing Nepalese society, a globalizing informal economy, and a transnationalizing social and cultural community. Race, ethnicity, gender, social class, nationality, immigration status, and citizenship status all intersected to influence women's domestic and service work in the United States. Women's agentic participation in diasporic networks and activities and in global civic engagement enabled women to survive exploitative working conditions, thrive 7,000 miles from their communities in Nepal, and shine on a transnational stage. Their active sociocultural and economic contributions take on added social and sociological importance as women's transnational migration continues to expand into the twenty-first century.

This book illustrated the fluid boundaries among the various kinds of work that the women were engaged in. As workers, as caregivers to their own and their employers' children, and as local and transnational community builders, Nepali migrant women were constantly engaged in labor that was both productive and reproductive. The women's work was exhausting, consisting of long days and nights in their paid jobs and time away from work packed with community activities and phone calls home. The work itself was often invisible, but its effects could clearly be seen in both the United States and Nepal. By moving beyond existing scholarship on racialized gendered labor in informal service and domestic work and by adding gender and gender perspectives to the transnational scholarship, this book makes three major contributions to the understanding of the multidimensional lives of immigrants/migrants in general, and Nepali women in particular.

First, this book tells us how middle-class Nepali women strategically took advantage of wage and status differentials between the United States and Nepal to improve their own lifestyle and contribute to their communities. They were able to do so because their gender made them attractive workers in the informal economy and because they did not experience their loss of occupational status to be incommensurate with their gender. They also were able to adapt to this loss of occupational status through their transnational contributions. Their move to the United States did not involve desperation but was a calculated and thoughtful choice, representing a break from the human capital and neoclassical theories of gender migration.

Second, this book tells us about the particular work experiences of transnational workers embedded in a pan-coethnic market, which is distinct from previous literature about workers who work for employers of another ethnicity *and* from studies of workers in a coethnic labor market. The cultural similarities and historical and current status differences between Nepali workers and Indian employers created unique tensions for these workers. Little research has been done on similar situations, but this concept could be applied in different contexts—for example, to Honduran migrant workers and Mexican American employers or to Vietnamese workers and their Korean employers in the United States.

Third, these women's economic contributions, which extended well beyond family and their sociocultural contributions to the diasporic community, add a new dimension to existing understandings of the term "transnationalism." Women were not just investing in themselves or their families—they were doing community-building work based on a sense of moral obligation and social responsibility. These women were connected to formal transnational organizations such as NGOs, but their community-building work also took place at an interpersonal level. Thus this book bridges studies of transnationalism from above and transnationalism from below to reveal the rich forms of participation that may occur right in the middle of transnational space.

To conclude, the women in this book held low-paying, low-status jobs, but the income this work generated enabled them to achieve recognition and respect in a broader transnational context. Women were isolated as individuals in the workplace, but as part of the Nepali diaspora they collectively built a transnational community. Women were not able to bring about an immediate change in their own work conditions, but through social, cultural, and economic transnational practices and civic engagement they changed the conditions of their lives in the United States and their communities in Nepal. Yes, women experienced marginalization in their work life, but marginalization should not be considered as the only experience of transnational women workers. For the Nepali women migrants in this book, the effects of their civic citizenship, agency, and empowerment were far-reaching, transcending global boundaries.

Appendix

◦

Glossary

◦

Works Cited

◦

Index

o　　o　　o

Appendix

Research Participants' Demographic and Socioeconomic Backgrounds

No	Demographic information: age, religion, caste, ethnicity	Education	Reason for Migration	Work in Nepal	Work in the US
1	42, Hindu, Chettri	MA	Personal and political	High school teacher in a private American school	Childcare
2	41, Hindu Chettri	MA	Professional visit	Coordinator, international student exchange program	Childcare
3	57, Hindu, Brahmin	MA	Personal and social	Bank officer	Childcare
4	40, Hindu, Chettri	MA	Personal	Accountant	Childcare
5	28, Buddhist, Tamang	MBA	Political and personal	NGO worker and teacher	Childcare and work in laundromat
6	47, Hindu, Newar	Nursing	Invitation from a friend	Nurse	Childcare (worked previously in a restaurant)
7	40, Hindu, Brahmin	BA	Personal and social	NGO Worker	Childcare
8	40, Hindu-Buddhist, Tamang	BA	Invitation from a friend	NGO Worker	Childcare and restaurant

No	Demographic information: age, religion, caste, ethnicity	Education	Reason for Migration	Work in Nepal	Work in the US
9	42, Hindu, Thakuri	BA	Invitation from a friend	High school teacher and NGO	Cashier in convenience store
10	43, Buddhist, Thakali	BA	Economic	Government job	Childcare
11	42, Hindu, Brahmin	BA	Social and personal	High school teacher and social worker	Childcare
12	54, Hindu, Newar	BA	To visit her son	High school teacher	Childcare
13	43, Hindu, Chettri	BA	To accompany husband	Founder of a high school and teacher in that school	Childcare
14	41, Hindu, Chettri	BA	Professional visit	High school teacher	Childcare
15	43, Buddhist, Gurung	BA	Social and personal	NGO Worker	Childcare and work in a jewellery shop
16	35, Hindu, Brahmin	BA	Economic	Teacher	Childcare
17	39, Hindu, Chettri	BA	Husband's education	Teacher	Childcare
18	51, Hindu, Newar	BA	Economic	Business owner	Childcare
19	40, Hindu, Chettri	BA	Personal and social	Teacher	Beauty salon
20	38, Hindu, Brahmin	BA	Business	Managing family business	Housecleaning
21	52, Hindu, Chettri	2-year college	Economic	Housewife	Childcare
22	50, Hindu, Chettri	2-year college	Economic and personal	Housewife	Childcare
23	50, Hindu Chettri	2-year college	To visit a son	Assisting family business	Convenience store and childcare

No	Demographic information: age, religion, caste, ethnicity	Education	Reason for Migration	Work in Nepal	Work in the US
24	41, Hindu-Buddhist, Thakali	2-year college	Political	Housewife	Childcare
25	48, Hindu-Buddhist, Newar	2-year college	To attend her brother's graduation	Teacher	Childcare
26	44, Hindu, Chettri	2-year college	Social	Public relations manager in a private company	Childcare and domestic
27	46, Hindu, Chettri	2-year college	To visit a family member	Administrative staff in a private company	Childcare and restaurant work
28	47, Hindu, Chettri	2-year college	Political	Teacher	Childcare and domestic
29	46, Buddhist, Gurung	High school	To attend a daughter's graduation	Housewife	Childcare
30	38, Buddhist, Gurung	High school	Political	Police	Coffee shop
31	39, Hindu, Chettri	High school	Political	Police	Restaurant work
32	46, Hindu, Brahmin	High school	Professional Visit	NGO worker	Childcare
33	47, Hindu, Chettri	High school	Diversity visa	Bank	Childcare and restaurant work
34	50, Hindu, Chettri	High school	Husband's education	Housewife	Childcare
35	50, Buddhist-Hindu, Gurung	No formal education	Economic	Housewife	Childcare, restaurant work, and beauty salon

.

Glossary

bartas: religious fasts

bhajan: religious songs

Brahmin: one of the highest-ranked castes in Nepal along with Kshatriya

Chettri: ethnic group

Dahar Khane: a female feast on Teej eve

daan: the Hindu religious practice of giving selflessly

Deepavali: the Hindu "festival of lights"; also spelled *Diwali* and *Devali* in certain South Asian regions

devanagari: the written alphabet in the languages of Nepal and India

dharma: Hindu/Buddhist practice of moral duty and responsibility

Durga Puja: a Hindu festival that celebrates the goddess Durga

Ganesh: one of the major Hindu gods (aka the god of obstacles)

Gurkhas: Nepali soldiers who served in the British and Indian armies starting in the nineteenth century; the tradition continues until the present day

Hindu: religious identity

Janma astami: Lord Krishana's birthday

jat: subcaste; there are thirty-six subcastes.

Kshatriya: the second-highest-ranked caste in Nepal

luxmi puja: worship of the goddess of wealth

ladoo: Indian/Nepali confection; ladoo is particularly offered to the Hindu god Ganesh

Nepali: a citizen of Nepal (noun); pertaining to Nepal's culture or language (adj.)

red pote: necklace made out of red beads that is traditionally worn by Hindu women until they become widows

puja: worship (a Sanskrit term)

Satya Narayan Puja: religious event that marks the worship of the god Bishnu

sewa: Hindu/Buddhist practice of service to others

Shree Krishna: Hindu god; one of the main characters of the sacred, oldest Hindu text *Shrimad Bhagavad Geeta*.

Teej: Hindu festival in which women gather and feast; on the second day women fast for their husband's longevity

varna: (lit., color of the skin) Ranking of people in a social order. Four main varna by hierarchy: Brahmin, Kshatriyas, Vaishyas, and Shudras.

o   o   o

Works Cited

Abrego, Leisy. 2009. "Economic Well-Being in Salvadoran Transnational Families: How Gender Affects Remittance Practices." *Journal of Marriage and Family* 71 no. 1: 1070–85.

Acharya, Meena. 2000. *Labour Market Development and Poverty: With Focus on Opportunities for Women in Nepal.* Kathmandu, Nepal: Tanka Prasad Acharya Memorial Foundation in cooperation with Friedrich-Ebert-Stiftung Foundation.

Acharya, Meena, and Lynn Bennett. 1981. *Rural Women in Nepal: An Aggregate Analysis and Summary of 8 Village Studies: The Status of Women in Nepal.* Kathmandu, Nepal: Center for Economic Development and Administration, Tribhuvan Univ.

Adhikaar. "What We Do." http://www.adhikaar.org/what-we-do/. Accessed April 21, 2013.

Alicea, Marixsa. 1997. "'A Chambered Nautilus': The Contradictory Nature of Puerto Rican Women's Role in the Social Construction of a Transnational Community." *Gender and Society* 11, no. 5: 597–626.

Anderson, Bridget. 2002. "Just Another Job?: The Commodification of Domestic Labor." In Ehrenrich and Hochschild, *Global Woman,* 104–14.

———. 2006. "Doing the Dirty Work?: The Global Politics of Domestic Labour." In Zimmerman, Litt, and Bose, *Global Dimensions of Gender and Carework,* 226–37.

Barker, Drucilla K., and Susan F. Feiner. 2010. "As the World Turns: Globalization, Consumption, and the Feminization of Work." *Rethinking Marxism* 22, no. 2: 246–52.

Basu, Subho. 2010. "Nepal: From Hindu Monarchy to Secular Democracy." In *Religion and Politics in South Asia,* edited by Ali Riaz, 98–118. London: Routledge.

Bhadra, Chandra. 1997. "Intra-Household Gender Analysis of Work Roles and Distribution of Resources: Pilot Study in a Nepalese Village." PhD diss., Oregon State Univ., Corvallis.

————. 2007. Revised January 2008. "International Labour Migration of Nepalese Women: The Impact of Their Remittances on Poverty Reduction." Asia Pacific Research and Training Network on Trade, Working Paper Series 44. http://www.unescap.org/tid/artnet/pub/wp4407.pdf. Accessed April 18, 2013.

————. 2009. "The State of Women in Nepal." *South Asian Journal*, no. 24: 80–88.

Billsborrow, Richard E., and Hania Zlotnik. 1991. "Preliminary Report of the UN Expert Group Meeting on the Feminization of Internal Migration." *International Migration Review* 26, no. 1: 138–61.

Blaikie, Piers, John Cameron, and David Seddon, eds. 2001. *Nepal in Crisis: Growth and Stagnation at the Periphery*. Delhi: Adroit Publishers.

Bohra-Mishra, Pratikshya. 2011. "Nepalese Migrants in the United States of America: Perspectives on their Exodus, Assimilation Pattern and Commitment to Nepal." *Journal of Ethnic and Migration Studies* 37, no. 9: 1527–37.

Brown, Irene, and Joya Misra. 2003. "The Intersection of Gender and Race in the Labor Market." *Annual Review of Sociology* 29, no 1: 487–513.

Cameron, Mary. 1998. *On the Edge of Auspicious: Gender and Caste in Nepal*. Urbana: Univ. of Illinois Press.

Carrasco, Lorena Nuñez. 2010. "Transnational Family Life among Peruvian Migrants in Chile: Multiple Commitments and the Role of Social Remittances." *Journal of Comparative Family Studies* 41, no. 2: 187–204.

Central Bureau of Statistics. 1996. 2001. *Statistical Pocket Book of Nepal*. Kathmandu, Nepal.

Chang, Grace. 2000. *Disposable Domestics: Immigrant Women Workers in the Global Economy*. Boston, MA: South End Press.

Ching Yoon Louie, Miriam. 2001. *Sweatshop Warriors: Immigrant Women Workers Take on the Global Economy*. Boston, MA: South End Press.

Choo, Hae Yeon, and Myra Marx Ferree. 2010. "Practicing Intersectionality in Sociological Research: A Critical Analysis of Inclusions, Interactions, and Institutions in the Study of Inequalities." *Sociological Theory* 28, no. 2: 129–49.

Chowdhury, Elora Halim. 2011. *Transnationalism Reversed: Women Organizing against Gendered Violence in Bangladesh*. Praxis: Theory in Action. New York: State Univ. of New York Press.

Colen, Shellee. 1986. "With Respect and Feeling: Voices of West Indian Child Care and Domestic Workers in New York City." In *All American Women: Lines That Divide, Ties That Bind*, edited by Johnetta B. Coe, 46–70. New York: Free Press.

Collins, Patricia Hill. 1990. *Black Feminist Thought: Knowledge, Consciousness and the Politics of Empowerment (Perspectives on Gender)*. London: Routledge.

———. 1991. "Learning from the Outsider Within." In Fonow and Cook, *Beyond Methodology,* 35–56.

Crenshaw, Kimberlie. 1991. "Mapping the Margins: Intersectionality, Identity, Politics, and Violence against Women of Color." *Stanford Law Review* 43, no. 6: 1241–99.

Da, Wei-Wei. 2010. "Support Networking Strategies of Female Chinese Immigrants in London, Ontario." *Asian and Pacific Migration Journal* 19, no. 4: 525–50.

Das Gupta, Monisha. 1997. "What Is Indian about You?: A Gendered, Transnational Approach to Ethnicity." *Gender and Society* 11, no. 5: 572–96.

———. 2008. "Housework, Feminism, and Labor Activism: Lessons from Domestic Workers in New York." *Signs: Journal of Women in Culture and Society* 33, no. 3: 532–37.

Desai, Manisha. 2002. "Transnational Solidarity: Women Agency, Structural Adjustment, and Globalization." In *Women's Activism and Globalization: Linking Local Struggles and Transnational Politics,* edited by Nancy Naples and Manisha Desai, 15–33. London: Routledge.

———. 2009. *Gender and the Politics of Possibilities: Rethinking Globalization.* Lanham, MD: Rowman & Littlefield.

Devault, Marjorie. 1999. *Liberating Method: Feminism and Social Research.* Philadelphia, PA: Temple Univ. Press.

Dhungel, Ramash Kumar. 1999. "Nepalese Immigrants in the United States of America." *Contributions to Nepalese Studies* 26: 119–34.

Diner, Hasia. 1983. *Erin's Daughters in America: Irish Immigrant Women in the Nineteenth Century.* Baltimore, MD: Johns Hopkins Univ. Press.

Dixit, Kanak Mani, and Shastri Ramachandaran, eds. 2002. *State of Nepal.* Nepal: Himal Books.

Domestic Workers United. "NY Domestic Workers Bill of Rights." www.domestic workersunited.org/campaigns.php. Accessed April 21, 2013.

Eckstein, Susan, and Thanh-Nghi Nguyen. 2011. "The Making and Transnationalization of an Ethnic Niche: Vietnamese Manicurists." *International Migration Review* 45, no. 3: 639–74.

Ehrenreich, Barbara, and Arlie Russell Hochschild, eds. 2002. *Global Woman: Nannies, Maids, and Sex Workers in the New Economy.* New York: Metropolitan Books.

Fernandez-Kelly, Maria Patricia. 1983. *For We Are Sold, I and My People: Women and Industry in Mexico's Frontier.* Berkeley: Univ. of California Press.

Fisher, James. 1986. *Trans-Himalayan Traders: Economy, Society, and Culture in Northwest Nepal.* Berkeley: Univ. of California Press.

Fix, Michael, and Wendy Zimmermann. 2001. "All Under One Roof: Mixed-Status Families in an Era of Reform." *International Migration Review* 35, no. 2: 397–419.

Fonow, Mary Margaret, and Judith A. Cook, eds. 1991. *Beyond Methodology: Feminist Scholarship as Lived Research.* Bloomington: Indiana Univ. Press.

Furer-Haimendorf, Christoph von. 1964. *The Sherpas of Nepal: Buddhist Highlanders.* London: John Murray.

Gamburd, Michele. 2003. "Breadwinner No More." In Ehrenreich and Hochschild, *Global Woman,* 190–206.

———. 2008. "Milk Teeth and Jet Planes: Kin Relations in Families of Sri Lanka's Transnational Domestic Servants." *City & Society* 20, no. 1: 5–31.

Gaughan, Joseph, and Louis Ferman. 1987. "Toward an Understanding of the Informal Economy." *The Annals of the American Academy of Political and Social Science* 493, no. 1: 15–25.

George, Sheba Matiam. 2005. *When Women Come First: Gender and Class in Transnational Migration.* Berkeley: Univ. of California Press.

Glenn, Evelyn Nakano. 1986. *Issei, Nisei, War Bride: Three Generations of Japanese American Women in Domestic Service.* Philadelphia, PA: Temple Univ. Press.

———. 1992. "From Servitude to Service Work: Historical Continuities in the Racial Division of Paid Work." *Signs: Journal of Women in Culture and Society* 18, no. 1: 1–43.

———. 2002. *Unequal Freedom: How Race and Gender Shape American Citizenship.* Cambridge, MA: Harvard Univ. Press.

Gurung, Harkha Bahadur. 1998. *Nepal: Social Demography and Expressions.* Kathmandu, Nepal: New ERA.

Hamal Gurung, Shobha. 2003. "Women in Factory-Based and Home-Based Carpet Production in Nepal: Beyond the Formal and Informal Economy." PhD diss., Northeastern Univ., Boston, MA.

———. 2004. "Women Weavers in Nepal: Between Global Market and Local Craft Production." In *The Power of Women's Informal Networks: Lessons in Societal Change from South Asia and West Africa,* edited by Bandana Purkayastha and Mangala Subramaniam, 89–104. Lanham, MD: Lexington Books.

———. 2008. "Growing Up Hindu: Mapping the Memories of a Nepali Woman in the United States." In Narayan and Purkayastha, *Living Our Religions,* 195–210.

———. 2010. "Nepali Female Migrants and Informalization of Service and Care Work: Service or Servitude?" *The Journal of Workplace Rights* 14, no. 3: 375–96.

———. 2014. "Sex Trafficking and the Sex Trade Industry: The Processes and Experiences of Nepali Women." *Journal of Intercultural Studies*, Special Issue: "Trafficking in Persons" 5, no. 2: 163–81.

———. 2014. "Shifting Gender Roles and Shifting Power Relations: Immigrant/ Migrant Nepali Families in New York and Los Angeles." In *Migration, Diaspora and Identity: Cross-National Experiences*, International Perspectives on Migration 6, edited by Georgina Tsolidis, 191–202. New York: Springer.

Hamal Gurung, Shobha, and Bandana Purkayastha. 2013. "Gendered Labor: Experiences of Nepali Women within Pan-Ethnic Informal Labor Markets in Boston and New York." In *Immigrant Women Workers in the Neoliberal Age*, edited by Nilda Flores-Gonzalez, Anna Romina Guevarra, Maura Toro-Morn, and Grace Chang, 81–116. Urbana: Univ. of Illinois Press.

Hangen, Susan. 2005. "Race and the Politics of Identity in Nepal." *Ethnology* 44, no. 1: 49–64.

Harding, Sandra. 1987. *Feminism and Methodology*. Bloomington: Indiana Univ. Press.

Harris, John, and Michael Todaro. 1970. "Migration, Unemployment, and Development: A Two-Sectoral Analysis." *American Economic Review* 60, no. 1: 126–42.

Henry, Stuart. 1982. "The Working Unemployed: Perspectives on the Informal Economy and Unemployment." *Sociological Review* 30, no. 3: 460–77.

Herd, Pamela, and Madonna Harrington Meyer. 2006. "Care Work: Invisible Civic Engagement." In Zimmerman, Litt, and Bose, *Global Dimensions of Gender and Carework*, 324–40.

Hondagneu-Sotelo, Pierrette. 2007. *Domestica: Immigrant Workers Cleaning and Caring in the Shadows of Affluence*. Berkeley: Univ. of California Press.

Hondagneu-Sotelo, Pierrette, and Ernestine Avila. 1997. "I'm Here but I'm There: The Meaning of Latina Transnational Motherhood." *Gender and Society* 11, no. 5: 548–71.

Horton, Sarah. 2009. "A Mother's Heart Is Weighed Down with Stones: A Phenomenological Approach to the Experience of Transnational Motherhood." *Culture, Medicine, and Psychiatry* 33, no. 1: 21–40.

Ignacio, Emily. 2005. *Building Diaspora: Filipino Community Formation on the Web*. New Brunswick, NJ: Rutgers Univ. Press.

Institute of International Education. 2014. "Top 25 Places of Origin of International Students, 2012/13–2013/14." Open Doors Report on International

Educational Exchange, http://www.iie.org/opendoors. http://www.iie.org /Research-and-Publications/Open-Doors/Data/International-Students/Lead ing-Places-of-Origin/2012-14.

Institute of Social Studies Trust. 2007. *Progress of Women in South Asia 2007*. New Delhi: India.

Jack, Dana Crowley, and Mark Van Ommeren. 2007. "Depression in Nepalese Women: Tradition, Changing Roles, and Public Health Policy." In Mogha-dam, *From Patriarchy to Empowerment*, 243–57.

Jafar, Afshan. 2011. *Women's NGOs in Pakistan*. New York: Palgrave Macmillan.

Kabeer, Naila. 2002. *The Power to Choose: Bangladeshi Garment Workers in London and Dhaka*. London: Verso.

Katuna, Barret. 2012. "The Human Rights Enterprise and Women's Rights Orga-nizing." *Societies without Borders* 7, no. 2: 236–53.

Kelkar, Maneesha. 2011. "South Asian Immigration in the United States: A Gen-dered Perspective." *Harvard Journal of Asian American Policy Review* 22, no. 1: 55–63.

Kibria, Nazli. 1990. "Power, Patriarchy, and Gender Conflict in the Vietnamese Immigrant Community." *Gender and Society* 4, no. 1: 9–24.

———. 1994. "Migration and Vietnamese American Women: Remaking Ethnic-ity." In Zinn and Dill, *Women of Color*, 247–61.

King, Deborah. 1988. "Multiple Jeopardy, Multiple Consciousness: The Context of a Black Feminist Ideology." *Signs* 14, no. 1: 42–72.

Kofman, Eleonore. 2000. "Beyond a Reductionist Analysis of Female Migrants in Global European Cities: The Unskilled, Deskilled, and Professional." In Marchand and Runyan, *Gender and Global Reconstructing*, 129–39.

Kusakabe, Kyoko, and Ruth Pearson. 2010. "Transborder Migration, Social Repro-duction and Economic Development: A Case Study of Burmese Women Workers in Thailand. *International Migration* 48, no. 6: 13–43.

Lal, C. K. 2002. "Cultural Flows across a Blurred Boundary." In Dixit and Ramach-andaran, *State of Nepal*, 100–118.

Lan, Phi-Chia. 2006. "Maid or Madam?: Filipina Migrant Workers and the Conti-nuity of Domestic Labor." In Zimmerman, Litt, and Bose, *Global Dimensions of Gender and Carework*, 266–73.

Lawoti, Mahendra. 2010. "Evolution and Growth of the Maoist Insurgency in Nepal." In Lawoti and Pahari, *Maoist Insurgency in Nepal*, 3–30.

Lawoti, Mahendra, and Anup Pahari, eds. 2010. *The Maoist Insurgency in Nepal: Revolution in the Twenty-First Century*. London: Routledge.

Levine, Andrew, dir. 2003. *The Day My God Died*. Hong Kong: Andrew Levine Productions.

Levitt, Peggy. 2001. *The Transnational Villagers*. Berkeley: Univ. of California Press.

———. 2007. *God Needs No Passport: Immigrants and the Changing American Religious Landscape*. New York: The New Press.

Louie, Miriam Ching Yoon. 2001. *Sweatshop Warriors: Immigrant Women Workers Take on the Global Factory*. Boston, MA: South End Press.

Manandhar, Narayan. 2000. "Nepal Labor Force Survey: Some Gender Issues." *Across* 4 (2000): 9.

Marchand, Marianne, and Anne Sisson Runyan, eds. 2000. *Gender and Global Restructuring: Sightings, Sites and Resistances*. New York: Routledge.

———. 2000. "Introduction: Feminist Sighting of Global Restructuring: Conceptualizations and Reconceptualization." In Marchand and Runyan, *Gender and Global Restructuring*, 1–22.

McCall, Leslie. 2005. "The Complexity of Intersectionality." *Signs: Journal of Women in Culture and Society* 30, no. 3: 1771–1800.

McHugh, Ernestine. 1989. "Concepts of the Person among the Gurungs of Nepal." *American Ethnologist* 16: 75–86.

Menjivar, Cecilia. 2000. *Fragmented Ties: Salvadoran Immigrant Networks in America*. Berkeley: Univ. of California Press.

Moghadam, Valentine M. 1999. "Gender and Globalization." *Journal of World System Research* 5, no. 2: 367–88.

———. 2005. *Globalizing Women: Transnational Feminist Networks*. Baltimore, MD: Johns Hopkins Univ. Press.

———, ed. 2007. *From Patriarchy to Empowerment: Women's Participation, Movements, and Rights in the Middle East, North Africa, and South Asia*. Syracuse, NY: Syracuse Univ. Press.

———. 2007. "Women's Empowerment: An Introduction and Overview." In Moghadam, *From Patriarchy to Empowerment*, 1–16.

Naples, Nancy. 1996. "A Feminist Revisiting of the Insider/Outsider Debate: The 'Outsider Phenomena' in Rural Iowa." *Qualitative Sociology* 19, no. 1: 83–106.

———. 2003. *Feminism and Method: Ethnography, Discourse Analysis, and Activist Research*. New York: Routledge, 2003.

Narayan, Anjana, and Bandana Purkayastha. 2008. "Introduction." In Narayan and Purkayastha, *Living Our Religions*, 1–22.

———, eds. 2008. *Living Our Religions: Hindu and Muslim South Asian American Women Narrate Their Experiences*. Sterling, VA: Kumarian.

Pahari, Anup Kumar. 1991. "Ties That Bind: Gurkhas in History." *Himal* (July/ August): 6–12.

———. 1995. "The Origins, Growth and Dissolution of Feudalism in Nepal: A Contribution to the Debate on Feudalism in Non-European Societies." PhD diss., Univ. of Wisconsin-Madison.

———. 2010. "Unequal Rebellions: The Continuum of 'People's War' in India and Nepal." In Lawoti and Pahari, *Maoist Insurgency in Nepal*, 195–216.

Parillo, Vincent N. 2008. *Encyclopedia of Social Problems*. Thousand Oaks, CA: Sage Publications.

Parreñas, Rachel. 2001. *Servants of Globalization: Women, Migration, and Domestic Work*. Palo Alto, CA: Stanford Univ. Press.

———. 2005. "Long Distance Intimacy: Class, Gender and Intergenerational Relations between Mothers and Children in Filipino Transnational Families." *Global Networks* 5, no. 4: 317–36.

Pascale, Celine Marie. 2007. *Making Sense of Race, Class, and Gender: Commonsense, Power, and Privilege in the United States*. New York: Routledge.

Pessar, Patricia. 1999. "Engendering Migration Studies." *American Behavioral Scientist* 42, no. 4: 577–600.

———. 2005. "Women's Political Consciousness and Empowerment in Local, National, and Transnational Contexts: Guatemalan Refugees and Returnees." *Identities* 7, no. 4: 461–500.

Piper, Nicola. 2004. "Rights of Foreign Workers and the Politics of Migration in South-East and East Asia. *International Migration* 42, no. 5: 71–91.

Portes, Alejandro. 1997. "Globalization from Below: The Rise of Transnational Communities." Princeton University, September. http://www.transcomm.ox .ac.uk/working%20papers/portes.pdf. Accessed April 25, 2011.

Portes, Alejandro, and Saskia Sassen. 1987. "Making It Underground." *American Journal of Sociology* 93, no. 1: 30–61.

Pradhan, Rajendra. 2002. "Ethnicity, Caste and a Pluralist Society." In Dixit and Ramachandaran, *State of Nepal*, 1–21.

Purkayastha, Bandana. 2005. *Negotiating Ethnicity: Second-Generation South Asian Americans Traverse a Transnational World*. New Brunswick, NJ: Rutgers Univ. Press.

Purkayastha, Bandana, and Ranita Ray. 2010. "South Asian Americans." In *Encyclopedia of Asian American Issues Today*, edited by Edith Chen, Wendy Ng, and Peter Chua, 51–64. New York: Greenwood Press.

Ramachandaran, Shastri. 2002. "Nepal as Seen in India." In Dixit and Ramachandaran, *State of Nepal*, 287–310.

Ranjeet, Bidya. 2008. "At the Crossroads of Religions: The Experiences of a Newar Woman in Nepal and the United States" In Narayan and Purkayastha, *Living Our Religions*, 81–96.

Ranjeet, Bidya, and Bandana Purkayastha. 2007. "A Minority within a Minority: Nepalese American Women and Domestic Violence." In *Body Evidence: Intimate Violence against South Asian Women in America*, edited by Shamita Das Gupta, 38–42. New Brunswick, NJ: Rutgers Univ. Press.

Reinharz, Shulamit. 1992. *Feminist Methods in Social Research*. New York: Oxford Univ. Press.

Rollins, Judith. 1985. *Between Women: Domestics and Their Employers*. Philadelphia, PA: Temple Univ. Press.

Rome, Sunny Harris. 2010. "Promoting Family Integrity: The Child Citizen Protection Act and Its implications for Public Child Welfare." *Journal of Public Child Welfare* 4, no. 3: 245–62.

Romero, Mary. 1992. *Maid in the U.S.A.* New York: Routledge.

———. 2006. "Unraveling Privilege: Workers' Children and the Hidden Costs of Paid Childcare." In Zimmerman, Litt, and Bose, *Global Dimensions of Gender and Carework*, 240–46.

———. 2007. "Conceptualizing the Latina Experience in Care Work." In *A Companion to Latina/o Studies*, edited by Juan Flores and Renato Rosaldo, 264–75. Malden, MA: Blackwell.

Sassen, Saskia. 2000. *The Global City*. Princeton, NJ: Princeton Univ. Press.

———. 2006. *Cities in a World Economy*. Thousand Oaks, CA: Pine Forge.

Schiller, Nina Glick, Linda Basch, and Cristina Blanc-Szanton, eds. 1992. *Towards a Transnational Perspective on Migration*. New York: New York Academy of Sciences.

———. 1995. "From Immigrant to Transmigrant: Theorizing Transnational Migration." *Anthropological Quarterly* 68, no. 1: 48–63.

Schmalzbauer, Leah. 2009. "Mexican Migration in the Rural Mountain West." *Gender and Society* 23, no. 6: 747–67.

Shah, Saubhagya. 2002. "From Evil State to Civil Society." In Dixit and Ramachandaran, *State of Nepal*, 137–60.

Shrestha, Nanda Raj. 1990. *Landless and Migration in Nepal*. Boulder, CO: Westview Press.

Siddiqui, Tasneem. 2001. *Transcending Boundaries: Labor Migration of Women from Bangladesh*. Dhaka, Bangladesh: The Univ. Press.

Smith, Dorothy E. 1989. *The Everyday World as Problematic: A Feminist Sociology*. Northeastern Series on Feminist Theory. Boston, MA: Northeastern Univ. Press.

Subedi, Prathiva. 1993. *Nepali Women Rising*. Kathmandu, Nepal: Sahayogi Press.

Tamang, Seira. 2002. "The Politics of 'Developing Nepali Women.'" In Dixit and Ramachandaran, *State of Nepal*, 161–75.

Thieme, Susan, and Simone Wyss. 2005. "Migration Patterns and Remittance Transfer in Nepal: A Case Study of Sainik Basti in Western Nepal." *International Migration* 43, no. 5: 59–98.

Todaro, Michael. 1976. *Internal Migration in Developing Countries: A Review of Theory, Evidence, Methodology and Research Priorities*. Geneva: International Labor Organization.

United Nations Development Programme (UNDP). 2010. *Nepal Human Development Report*. Kathmandu, Nepal.

Upadhya, Sanjay. 2002. "A Dozen Years of Democracy: The Games That Parties Play." In Dixit and Ramachandaran, *State of Nepal*, 39–61.

US Department of Homeland Security. 2004. 2008. *Yearbook of Immigration Statistics*. Washington, DC: US Department of Homeland Security.

Wallerstein, Immanuel. 2004. *World-System Analysis: An Introduction*. Durham, NC: Duke Univ. Press.

Ward, Kathryn. 1990. "Introduction and Overview." In *Women Workers and Global Restructuring*, edited by Kathryn Ward, 1–22. Ithaca, NY: Cornell Univ. Press.

Waters, Mary, and Peggy Levitt, eds. 2002. *The Changing Face of Home: Transnational Lives of the Second Generation*. New York: Sage Books.

Watkins, Joanne. 1995. *Spirited Women: Gender, Religion, and Cultural Identity in the Nepal Himalaya*. New York: Columbia Univ. Press.

Wichterich, Christa. 2000. *The Globalized Woman: Reports from a Future of Inequality*. New York: Zed.

World Bank. 2011. *Migration and Remittances Factbook 2011*. http: data.worldbank .org/data-catalog/migration-and-remittances.

Yamanaka, Keiko. 2000. "Nepalese Labor Migration to Japan: From Global Warriors to Global Workers." *Ethnic and Racial Studies* 23, no. 1: 62–93.

Yuval-Davis, Nira. 1997. *Gender and Nation*. London: Sage Publications.

Zavella, Patricia. 1992. "Feminist Insider Dilemmas: Constructing Ethnic Identity with 'Chicana' Informants." *Frontiers* 13, no. 3: 53–76.

Zimmerman, Mary K., Jacquelyn S. Litt, and Christine E. Bose, eds. 2006. *Global Dimensions of Gender and Carework*. Stanford, CA: Stanford Social Sciences.

Zinn, Maxine Baca. 1979. "Field Research in Minority Communities: Ethical, Methodological, and Political Observations by an Insider." *Social Problems* 27, no. 2: 209–18.

Zinn, Maxine Baca, and Bonnie Thornton Dill. 1994. "Difference and Domination." In Zinn and Dill, *Women of Color*, 3–12.

———, eds. 1994. *Women of Color in U.S. Society*. Philadelphia, PA: Temple Univ. Press.

Zontini, Elisabetta. 2004. "Immigrant Women in Barcelona: Coping with the Consequences of Transnational Lives." *Journal of Ethnic and Migration Studies* 30, no. 6: 1113–44.

Index

Italic page numbers denote tables.

Abbrego, Leisy, 114–15
ABC/Nepal, 34n14
Abha (study participant): activism of,
    134–35; on being income earner, 110;
    codependence with, 77–78; on her
    employers, 145; reasons for migration
    by, 41; on religion, 56; transnational
    practices of, 118
abuse, 11, 34, 59, 80. *See also* emotional
    abuse
accusations of stealing, 66–67, 144
Acharaya, Meena, 86
activism: empowerment and, 133–36;
    engagement with, 2–3; in Nepal,
    26, 35; studies of, 113; transna-
    tional, 14–15, 16–17, 133–36, 139,
    146–47, 148
Adhikaar, 136–37, 137n7, 147
African Americans, 82
agency: effects of, 151; human rights and,
    115; labor exploitation and, 149; reli-
    gion and, 125–26; social capital and,
    4–5; studies of, 113; transnationalism
    and, 15–16n9, 15–17, 113, 129–33; trans-
    national practices and, 2–3, 124–29,
    146–47, 148
American families, 61–62, 61n3, 79, 79–80,
    83n6

American lifestyle, 104, 104n6, 106–7
Anita (study participant), 131–33, 135
Arab nations, 34
Australia, 30–31
autonomy, 133, 135–36, 135n4

babysitters. *See* childcare providers
Bangladesh, 11n8, 29, 32
bartas (religious fasts), 108, 159
Basch, Linda, 124–25
Basu, Subho, 26
beauty salons, 50, 67
Bennett, Lynn, 86
*Between Women: Domestics and Their
    Employers* (Rollins), 10, 144
Bhadra, Chandra, 8, 35, 48, 85, 100
bhajan, 124, 159
Bijaya (study participant), 130–31, 135
Binta (study participant), 69
Blanc-Szanton, Cristina, 124–25
Bohra-Mishra, Pratikshya, 31
Bollywood films, 56
Brahmins, 107–8, 159
breadwinners. *See* economic support;
    primary income earners
British Raj, 27–29
brothels, 34, 34n14

Brunei Darussalam, 30
Buddhism, 123, 123n1

Cameron, Mary, 87, 99
Canada, 30, 31, 97
care work. *See* childcare providers
"Care Work: Invisible Civic Engagement" (Herd and Meyer), 138
Caribbean migrants, 10, 82, 143
carpet production, 32–33, 99–100, 135n4, 146
Carrasco, Lorena Nuñez, 105
cashiers, 46, 46n1, 73, 75
caste: gender roles and, 86–87; Indians vs. Nepalis on, 69–70, 69–70n4; *jat*, 23, 159; in Nepal, 24, 25, 25n4, 26; of research participants, 155–57
Center for Governance, 87
Central American migrants, 143
Chettri ethnicity, 103, 107–8, 159
Chicanas, 82
childcare providers: backgrounds of, 77; codependence with, 76–78; domestic work by, 61, 62–63, 64–65, 83; downward occupational mobility and, 50; employment patterns of, 46, 46n1; exploitation of, 61; globalization and, 48; labor relations and, 72; live-in, 37, 55–56, 60, 61; narratives of, 1, 51, 76–78; prejudice and, 71; racism and, 59; reasons for working as, 47; recruiting replacement workers for, 53n5; stereotypes of, 142n1; traditional gender expectations and, 2; work conditions for, 10–11, 58, 62–66, 74–75, 143–44
children: education for, 42–43, 119–22; orphan, 16, 119; physical separation from, 88–93, 91n2, 92n3
Chinese migrants, 97, 128

Chowdhury, Elora Halim, 113, 148
citizenship status. *See* immigration status
civic engagement: agency and, 149; boundaries between local and global in, 138; effects of, 151; empowerment and, 21; religious values and, 123; transnational practices and, 115–18, 129–33
civil rights, 136–37, 147
civil war, 25–26, 143
clan-based rule, 24
class. *See* social class
classical migration studies, 7, 86
cleaning. *See* domestic workers; household tasks
codependence, 76–80
coethnic labor market. *See* pan-coethnic labor market
coethnic social networks. *See* social networks
coffee shops, 50, 50n3
colonialism, 71
combined workers, 72, 83
communication, transnational mothering and, 90
community building: agency and, 124–29; diasporic, 3, 115, 126, 127, 139, 150; importance of, 21; participation in, 16; transnationalism and, 15–16, 113–39, 140
community health clinic, 116–17
conjugal relationships, 92–97, 105, 109–10
convenience stores, 41–42, 50, 50n3
cooking: by childcare providers, 65, 67, 77; family gender roles and, 101–3, 104, 106, 108. *See also* food; household tasks
core and dependency framework (Wallerstein), 55
cross-national comparison, of labor migrants, 82
cultural capital, 52, 53–57, 76–78, 81, 83

cultural events. *See* sociocultural events and practices

culture, 11, 43–44

Da, Wei-Wei, 97

daan (giving), 122–23, 159

Dahar Khane, 126, 159

Das Gupta, Monisha, 10–11, 12, 13

Day My God Died, The (documentary), 34n15

decision making: empowerment of, 133; multiple factors in, 22–23, 36–45, 141, 142; political factors in, 40–41, 42–43; primary income earners and, 146; socioeconomic factors in, 31, 35–36n17, 37–41, 43–44, 45, 143; staying in the US and, 142–43; transnational practices and, 135–36

Deepavali, 55, 159

democracy, 25–26, 27, 29–30

demographics, 45, *155–57*

depression, 107

"Depression in Nepalese Women: Tradition, Changing Roles, and Public Health Policy" (Jack and Ommeren), 107

Desai, Manisha, 113, 148

Devanagari script, 55, 159

dharma (moral and religious duty), 122–23, 159

diaspora: author's participation in, 6; coethnic labor market and, 56–57; community building in, 3, 115, 126, 127, 139, 150; employers and workers in, 78; Indians vs. Nepalis in, 78; Levitt on, 15

discrimination, 26n7, 34n16, 72, 85–86. *See also* inequalities; race and racism

Diversity Visa (DV) Program, 3n5, 32, 32n13, 43, 50

division of labor, 94, 101–5, 104n5

Dolpo people, 86

domestic workers: childcare providers as, 61, 62–63, 64–65, 83; cross-national comparison of, 82; downward occupational mobility and, 8–9, 49–50; emotional abuse of, 34; employment patterns in, 46, 46n1, 48; exploitation of, 10, 144; Filipina, 9, 10–11; globalization and, 48; increasing demand for, 8; labor relations and, 72; live-in, 55–56, 97; men as, 112; as mobile workers, 73; racism and, 59, 68; socioeconomic status and, 143; stereotypes of, 142n1; white employers and, 83n6; work conditions for, 10–11, 75, 143–44; workplace rights for, 136–37, 137n7, 147–48

Domestic Workers Bill of Rights (New York State), 147

Domestic Workers United, 137n7, 147, 148

Dominican migrants, 115

downward occupational mobility: domestic workers and, 8–9, 49–50; economic support and, 134, 135; experiences of, 9, 74; gender roles and, 95–96, 150; informal work sector and, 9, 49–50, 52, 57; professional occupational fields and, 36, 49–50, 57, 142, 147; transnational practices and, 15, 118

dual workers, 72, 83

Durga (Goddess), 56

Durga Puja, 55, 159

DV (Diversity Visa) Program, 3n5, 32, 32n13, 43, 50

economic development, 29, 48

economic factors. *See* socioeconomic factors

economic support: changing view of
migrant women and, 3, 3n4; downward occupational mobility and, 134,
135; empowerment and, 133–36; examples of, 116–18, 130–33, 136; for family
and nonfamily, 114–15, 138, 146–47,
150; fund-raising and, 115, 129–33, 135;
gender roles and, 12–13, 16, 21; Levitt
on, 16n10; maintaining ties with Nepal
and, 114; patterns of, 16; percentage of
income for, 115–16; reasons for migration and, 37–39; for religious events
and organizations, 119–20, 122–24, 125;
for social organizations, 119–24, 138,
146–47; for sociocultural events, 14, 114,
125–29, 150; transnational networks
and, 120; for transnational practices,
115–18. *See also* primary income earners; remittance money
education: for children of migrants,
42–43, 119–22; college, 31, 36; gender
expectations and, 1–2; of Indians,
78; informal work sector and, 5–6,
8–9; labor market and, 4–5; in Nepal,
42–43, 91n2; of research participants,
155–57; transnational mothering and,
91, 91n2; in US, 49
emotional abuse: cross-national comparison of, 82; of domestic workers,
34; experiences of, 60, 66–67; labor
relations and, 81–82; pan-ethnic labor
market and, 11–12
employee-employer relationships. *See*
labor relations
employers: autonomy of, 60, 60n1; Nepali
migrants as, 54–55n6; power relations
with, 21; research methodology and,
18; Southeast Asian, 20, 47. *See also*
Indian employers; labor exploitation;
labor relations; work conditions

employment patterns: in beauty salons,
50; in coethnic labor market, 81, 83n6;
in coffee shops, 50, 50n3; in convenience stores, 50, 50n3; in informal
work sector, 2, 44, 46, 46n1, 48, 50,
50n3, 83; in Nepal, 46, *155–57*; for
restaurant workers, 50, 50n3
empowerment: achievement of, 5, 21;
agency and, 138, 147; effects of, 151;
feminist scholarship on, 6; gender
roles and, 110, 111; informal work
sector and, 143–45; transnationalism
and, 13–17, 21, 112, 133–36, 147. *See also*
power relations
English language, 36n19, 56
entertainment, 55, 56, 77
ethnicity: gender roles and, 86–87, 103;
intersectional framework and, 143–45;
multilayered, 14; prejudice against,
69–70n4, 72; of research participants,
155–57
ethnography, 5, 6, 17, 18, 109
Europe, 10, 31
everyday/everynight lived experience, 6
everyday lives, 4, 13, 21, 40, 123, 133
exploitation. *See* labor exploitation
eyebrow design specialists, 46

familial roles, 77–78, 80
family lives: codependence and, 77–78;
conjugal relationships and, 92–97,
105; engagement with, 5; examples
of, 94–97; gender roles and, 87–88;
immigration policies and, 87–88, 94;
of live-in workers, 97; reasons for
migration and, 40; reconfiguring, 13;
transnational structures of, 87–88;
women as primary income earners
and, 97–99

farms, 32, 33, 41

feminism, 7, 13, 16

feminization: of labor market, 7, 111; of labor migration, 22–23, 48, 140–41; of poverty, 8

Ferman, Louis, 57

Fernandez-Kelly, Maria Patricia, 105

Filipinas, 9, 10–11, 92, 105, 115, 125

Fisher, James, 86

F1 Student visas, 6n6

food: culture and, 126, 127; farming for, 41; sharing, 19; similarities with employers, 62, 76–77, 81, 145. *See also* cooking

free trade, 7, 25, 90

F2 visas, 2

fund-raising, 115, 129–33, 135

Gamburd, Michele, 105

Ganesh, 67, 159

gardening work, 65

Gaughan, Joseph, 57

GBNC (Greater Boston Nepalese Community), 3, 131

gender: in classical migration studies, 7; informal work sector and, 149; intersectional framework and, 58–60, 82, 143–45; transnational studies and, 15

gender discrimination, 26n7, 34n16, 85

gender identity, 99

gender roles, 84–112; adaptation of, 111–12, 112n9, 145–46; changes in, 12–13; division of labor and, 94; downward occupational mobility and, 95–96, 150; economic support and, 12–13, 16, 21; ethnicity and, 86–87, 103; expectations of, 1–2, 3, 3n4, 5; globalization and, 13, 48, 97, 111; Hinduism and, 86, 107–8, 108n7; household tasks and,

101–5, 104n5; as incentive to migrate, 40, 44, 142–43; intersectional framework and, 143–45; patriarchy and, 106–8, 109; power relations and, 5, 100–105, 100n4, 110; primary income earners and, 84, 94, 97–100, 105, 107, 111, 112; religion and, 107–8, 108n7; renegotiated, 109; traditional Nepali, 2, 85–87, 106–8, 112n9, 141, 145–46; transnationalism and, 13, 15–17, 87–88; transnational mothering and, 88–93, 91n2, 92n3

geographical movement. *See* migration patterns

George, Sheba Matiam, 109, 128–29

Gina (study participant), 39–40, 45, 99, 141, 142

giving (*daan*), 122–23, 159

Glenn, Evelyn Nakano, 10

global citizens, 129–33, 138, 151

globalization: gendered effects of, 13, 48; gender roles and, 13, 48, 97, 111; informal work sector and, 7–9, 48; migration patterns and, 7–9, 20, 22–23; reasons for migration and, 45; transnational mothering and, 90; women as primary income earners and, 97–99

Global North, 7–8, 34n15, 48

global restructuring, 7–8

Global South, 7–8, 10–11, 48, 141

God Needs No Passport: Immigrants and the Changing American Religious Landscape (Levitt), 124

Greater Boston Nepalese Community (GBNC), 3, 131

green cards, 78–79, 87–88, 95, 97

Grenada migrants, 125

Gurkhas, 27, 27n8, 28n9, 159

Gurung, 86

Haiti migrants, 125

Hamal Gurung, Shobha, 6n6, 87

Hays, Sharon, 92

head migrants. *See* lead migrants

Help Nepal, 5, 129, 148

Hema (study participant), 41–42, 51,
126–27, 135

Herd, Pamela, 138

Hindi language, 55

Hinduism: coethnic labor market and, 55;
core beliefs of, 122–23; as culture and
as religion, 108n, 108n8; definition of,
159; division of labor and, 103; gender
roles and, 86, 107–8, 108n7; in Nepal,
23–24, 25; simultaneous practice with
Buddhism, 123, 123n1

Hondagneu-Sotelo, Pierrette, 82, 83n6,
90

Horton, Sarah, 90–91

housecleaning. *See* domestic workers;
household tasks

household subsistence economy, 33

household tasks, 101–5, 104n5

human capital theory, 7, 29, 44, 74

human rights, 26, 27, 115, 136–37, 147–48.
See also civil rights; workplace rights

husbands. *See* migrant men

identity: gender, 99; national, 69, 81, 114;
Nepali, 3, 15, 127; occupational, 49;
religious, 108n8; South Asian regional,
47, 54, 81

Immigration Act of 1990 (US), 32

immigration policies, 54, 82, 82n5, 87–88,
94

immigration status: importance of, 68;
Indian employers and, 54, 78–79;
informal work sector and, 50, 52, 57;
intersectional framework and, 58–60,

82, 143–45; labor relations and, 64, 83;
personal factors and, 6, 6n6

income earners. *See* economic support;
primary income earners

India: British Raj in, 27–29; immigrants
from, 54–55; migration to, 28–29,
28n10, 30, 55; relations with Nepal, 55,
71; sex trafficking and, 34, 34n14

Indian employers: vs. American families,
79–80; codependence with, 76–80;
definition of, 11n8; immigration status
of, 54, 78–79; informal work sector
and, 54–57; labor exploitation by,
61–67, 81; labor relations with, 76–80,
81, 144–45, 150; prejudice of, 69–72;
shared language and, 55, 76–77, 79, 81,
145; stereotypes of nationality and, 69.
See also pan-coethnic labor market

Indians, 54, 69–70, 69–70n4, 78

inequalities: gender-based, 26n7, 34n16,
85; political, 45; structural, 24–25,
25n4, 26, 26n7

informal work sector, 20, 46–57; attraction
to, 50–51; challenges and pitfalls of,
58–83; cultural capital and, 52, 53–57,
81, 83; definition of, 48; downward
occupational mobility and, 9, 49–50,
52, 57; educated migrant women in,
5–6, 8–9; employment patterns in, 2,
44, 46, 46n1, 48, 50, 50n3, 83; gender
and, 149; globalization and, 7–9,
48; Global South and, 10–11; intersectionality of, 58–60, 82, 143–45,
149; as last resort, 52–53, 142; for
men, 92, 112; in Nepal, 33; personal
factors in selection of, 47, 57; social
and transnational networks in, 47,
53n4, 57, 60, 60n1, 64; social networks
and, 47, 51–53, 53n4, 57, 60, 60n1, 64;
Southeast Asian migrants in, 9, 53–57;

structural factors in, 46–47, 48–49, 57, 67–68; transnational networks and, 50–53; wage differentials and, 98. *See also* pan-coethnic labor market; work conditions

infrastructure, 29

INGOs (International Non-Governmental Organizations), 26, 30

insider status, 19

Institute of International Education, 31

internal migration patterns, 29, 32–33

International Non-Governmental Organizations (INGOs), 26, 30, 33–34, 35

intersectionality: of income earners and gender, 87; of the informal work sector, 58–60, 82, 143–45, 149; labor exploitation and, 59, 82; pan-coethnic labor market and, 9–12

interviews, 18–19, 18n11, 19n12

Jack, Dana Crowley, 107, 113

Jang Bahadur, 24

Janma astami, 125, 159

Japan, 30

jat, 23, 159

Kabita (study participant): accusations of stealing, 66–67, 144; emotional abuse of, 66–67; family life of, 94; as mobile worker, 73; on public transportation, 52; reasons for migration and, 42–43

Kanti (study participant), 102

karma, 16

Katuna, Barret, 113, 115

Kelkar, Maneesha, 82

Keralite immigrants, 109, 128–29

Kibria, Nazli, 13, 109–10, 128

Kiran (study participant), 120–23

Koirala, B. P., 24

Kshatriya, 159

labor conditions. *See* work conditions

labor exploitation, 143–45; agency and, 149; cross-national comparison of, 82; domestic workers and, 10, 144; examples of, 61–67; intersectional framework and, 59, 82; labor relations and, 81–82; pan-coethnic labor market and, 11–12, 61–67, 81; pan-ethnic labor market and, 11–12; prejudice and, 70–71; psychological, 144; racism as, 69; by Rana regime, 24; sex trafficking and, 34, 34nn14–16; types of, 60–61, 61n2

labor market: educated migrant women in, 4–5; feminization of, 7, 111; inconsistent social status in, 9; in Nepal, 29, 33–34. *See also* pan-coethnic labor market

labor migration: cross-national comparison of, 82; feminization of, 22–23, 48, 140–41; gender discrimination in, 34n16; historical context for, 27–32; in India, 55; neoclassical theory of, 7, 44; push and pull factors in, 22, 34–35, 44–45

labor relations, 60–65; examples of, 61–67, 143–45; familial roles and, 78; immigration status and, 78–79, 83; with Indian employers, 76–80, 81, 144–45, 150; lack of control over, 72; preference and discrimination in, 68–72; in service work, 75–76; sociocultural factors in, 80; structural factors in, 68. *See also* labor exploitation; work conditions

labor rights. *See* workplace rights

ladoo, 67, 159

lahur, 28n9

lahure, 28n9

language: English, 36n19, 56; Hindi, 55; India and, 28; Indian employers and, 55, 76–77, 79, 81, 145; Nepali, 19, 55, 137n7

Lata (study participant), 73

Latinas: cross-national comparison of, 82; as domestic workers, 10; exploitation of, 82, 144; similarities and differences with, 4; transnational mothering and, 92; work conditions for, 143

Lawoti, Mahendra, 25n4

leadership, 2–3, 16, 125, 131, 139

lead migrants, 5–6, 13, 41–44, 87–88, 140–41. *See also* primary income earners

legal migrants, 4

Levine, Andrew, 34n15

Levitt, Peggy, 13–15, 115, 124–29, 133

lifestyle, American, 104, 104n6, 106–7

lived experiences, 6, 18, 21, 22, 60, 149

live-in workers, 37, 55–56, 60, 61, 97

lone migrants. *See* lead migrants

luxmi puja, 125, 159

Mahendra, 24

Maiti Nepal, 34n14

Making Sense of Race, Gender, and Class (Pascale), 10

Mala (study participant), 51

Manju (study participant), 89

Maoists, 25–27, 30, 35, 40–41

Marchand, Marianne, 7

marginalization, 10, 72, 80, 82, 85, 151

marriage, 2, 43–44, 108. *See also* conjugal relationships; family lives

matrix of domination, 10

Maya (study participant): accusations of stealing, 67, 144; coethnic social

networks and, 51–52; on household tasks, 102–3; on obtaining work, 52–53; on work conditions, 67

Meena (study participant), 51, 64–65, 76–77, 110, 135

Meeta (study participant), 126

Mexico and Mexicans, 10, 89–90, 105, 150

Meyer, Madonna Harrington, 138

middle-class status: education for, 91n2; gender roles and, 109–10; household tasks and, 101, 106; migration patterns and, 141–42, 143; studies of, 14–15; wage differentials and, 149–50

migrant men: childcare by, 92; conjugal relationships and, 92–97, 105, 109–10; historical context for, 27, 28; household tasks and, 101–5; informal work sector and, 112; as *lahure*, 28n9; as mobile workers, 100–101, 100n4; return to Nepal by, 94, 95. *See also* family lives; patriarchy

migrants, lead, 13, 41–44, 87–88, 140–41

migrant women: backgrounds of, 36–37, 36nn18–19, 142–43, 142n1; definition of, 2n2; demographic information, 155–57; educated, 1–2, 4–5, 8–9; as lead migrants, 5–6, 13, 41–44, 87, 140–41; legal, 4; reasons for migration by, 8–9, 32–36, 34–35, 35–36n17, 35–41, 155–57; similarities and differences between, 4; as students, 2n1

Migration and Remittances Factbook 2011 (World Bank), 30–31

"Migration and Vietnamese American Women: Remaking Ethnicity" (Kibria), 128

migration, definition of, 3n5

migration patterns: feminization of, 13, 140–41; globalization and, 7–9, 20,

22–23; historical context of, 27–32, 28n10; internal, 29, 32–33; shift in, 2, 3, 5–6. *See also* labor migration

migration studies, 7, 110

mobile workers: definition of, 72; husbands as, 100–101, 100n4; reasons for changing jobs by, 68, 83; socioeconomic factors for, 87; work conditions and, 72, 73

Moghadam, Valentine M., 113, 148

monarchy, 24–25, 27

Mongol, 69–70n4

moral and religious duty (*dharma*), 122–23, 159

Moroccans, 97

mothers and mothering: conjugal relationships and, 43; construction of motherhood, 88; intensive mothering, 92; remittance money from, 114–15; roles of mothers, 2; single mothers, 45, 91, 117; transnational mothering, 88–93, 91n2, 92n3, 111

Naina (study participant), 106

nannies. *See* childcare providers

National Domestic Workers Alliance, 137n7, 147

national identity, 69, 81, 114

nationality: in coethnic labor market, 68–72; Indians vs. Nepalis on, 69–70, 69–70n4; intersectional framework and, 58–60, 82, 143–45; stereotypes of, 68–69

Neera (study participant), 120

Negotiating Ethnicity (Purkayastha), 14

neoclassical theory, 7, 44

Nepal: activism in, 26, 35; buying property in, 115; civil war in, 25–26, 143; education in, 42–43, 91n2; employment in, 46, *155–57*; eventual return to, 136, 136n5; Hinduism in, 23–24, 25; human rights in, 115; husbands return to, 94, 95; image of, 68–69; labor force in, 33–34; maintaining connections to, 114–15, 138; modern history of, 23–27; nationality, religion, and caste in, 69–70, 69–70n4; patriarchy in, 85–87, 145–46; poverty and, 70–71; professional occupational fields in, 46, 143; relations with India, 55, 71; structural inequality in, 24–25, 25n4, 26; traditional gender roles in, 85–87, 106–8, 112n9, 141, 145–46; women religious practitioners in, 125; women's movement in, 26, 35, 85–86, 143

Nepali, definition of, 159

Nepali identity, 3, 15, 127

Nepali language, 19, 55, 137n7

Nepali migrants: as employers, 54–55n6; historical context for, 27–32, 28n10; in professional occupational fields, 33–34, 46, 49, 54–55n6, 143; reasons for migration and, 30; statistics on, 31, 34; top destinations for, 30–31; to US, 31–32, 31n12, 35–36. *See also* migrant men; migrant women

Nepali migrant women. *See* migrant women

Nepali Women's Global Network (NWGN), 5, 115, 129, 148

networks. *See* social networks; transnational networks

NGOs. *See* nongovernmental organizations

Nira (study participant), 99

Nitu (study participant), 96–97

nongovernmental organizations (NGOs):
economic support for, 117–18; engagement with, 2–3, 14–15, 35, 129–33, 148;
labor force in, 33–34; in Nepal, 26, 30;
role of, 21; on sex trafficking, 34n14;
transnational networks and, 30, 41
nurses/nursing, 49, 109, 117–18
NWGN (Nepali Women's Global Network), 5, 115, 129, 148

occupational ghettoization, 10
occupational identity, 49
occupational mobility. See downward
occupational mobility
Ommeren, Mark Van, 107
orphans, 16, 119

paid workers. See economic support;
primary income earners
Pakistan, 11n8, 32, 67
Panchayat system, 24–25
pan-coethnic labor market, 11–12, 20;
advantages and disadvantages of,
12; diaspora and, 56–57; downward
occupational mobility and, 49–50;
educated migrant women in, 4–5;
employment patterns in, 81, 83n6;
experiences of, 150; gender roles and,
92; informal work sector and, 53–57;
labor exploitation and, 11–12, 61–67,
81; prejudice in, 68–72; stereotypes of
nationality in, 68–69; transnational
networks and, 144–45; undocumented
workers and, 53; women as primary
income earners and, 97–99; work
conditions in, 62–67, 68. See also Indian
employers
Parillo, Vincent N., 72

Parreñas, Rachel, 9, 115
Pascale, Celine Marie, 10
patriarchy: gender roles and, 106–8, 109;
household tasks and, 101; in Nepal,
85–87, 145–46; primary income earners and, 96, 106–7; supporting and
subverting simultaneously, 21, 106–8
People's Movement, 25–27, 30, 35, 40–41, 85
permanent residency cards. See green
cards
personal factors: in choosing informal
work sector, 47, 57; in migration decisions, 37–41, 42, 43–44, 45
Pessar, Patricia, 105, 110
political asylum, 8, 22, 50, 89
political factors, in migration decisions,
40–41, 42–44, 45
Portes, Alejandro, 13, 14
pote, 108, 159
poverty, 8, 35, 35–36n17, 70–71
power relations, 21; changes in, 12–13;
gender roles and, 5, 100–105, 100n4,
110; primary income earners and,
99–101, 100n4, 110; transnationalism
and, 133–36; unequal, 81–82
prejudice, 68–72, 81
primary income earners: decision making and, 146; division of labor and,
94; gender roles and, 84, 94, 97–100,
105, 107, 111, 112; intersection with
gender, caste, and social class, 87; lead
migrants as, 13, 41–44, 87–88, 140–41;
legal migrants as, 4; mothering and,
92; patriarchy and, 96, 106–7; power
relations and, 99–101, 100n4, 110
Prithvi Narayan, 23
privatization, 25
Priya (study participant), 40, 45, 119–20
professional occupational fields: conjugal
relationships and, 97; downward

occupational mobility and, 36, 49–50, 57, 142, 147; husbands' loss of, 94; Indians and, 54; participation in, 33–34, 46, 49, 54–55n6, 143; reasons for migration and, 39, 42–43
psychological exploitation, 144
public transportation, 52
puja, 124, 125, 125n2, 159
Purkayastha, Bandana, 31, 78
push and pull factors, 22, 34, 44–45, 141

Qatar, 30
questionnaires, end-of-interview, 18–19, 18n11
quitting jobs, 72, 144

race and racism: Indians vs. Nepalis on, 69–70, 69–70n4; intersectional framework and, 58–60, 82, 143–45; negotiation of, 14; in pan-coethnic labor market, 68–72
Rama (study participant), 101–2
Rana regime (1846–1950), 24, 27, 29
Rani (study participant), 73
Ray, Ranita, 31, 78
recruiting replacement workers, 53, 53n5, 83
red pote, 108, 159
refugees/asylees, 8, 22, 50, 52, 89
religion: agency and, 125–26; gender roles and, 107–8, 108n7; Indian employers and, 56; Indians vs. Nepalis on, 69–70, 69–70n4; of research participants, 155–57; women practitioners of, 125
religious events and organizations: economic support for, 114, 119–20, 122–24, 125; importance of, 128–29
religious fasts (*bartas*), 108, 159

religious identity, 108n8
remittance money: to family and nonfamily, 114–15, 138; gender roles and, 16; historical context for, 28; importance of, 98–99; from mothers, 114–15; narratives of, 116–18; patterns of, 16, 16n10, 115–16, 123–24; transnational mothering and, 90; women as lead migrants and, 41–44. *See also* economic support; primary income earners
research methodology, 17–20, 19n12
research participant demographics, 155–57
restaurant workers, 46, 46n1, 50, 50n3, 73
Rita (study participant), 75, 78–79, 103–5, 104n5
Rollins, Judith, 10, 72, 82, 144
Romero, Mary, 10, 82
Runyan, Anne Sisson, 7

Sakhi for South Asian Women, 11, 11n7
salaries, 61, 62, 63, 79. *See also* economic support; primary income earners
Salvadorans, 90–91
Sarina (study participant), 74–75
Satya Narayan Puja, 125, 159
Saudi Arabia, 30
Schiller, Nina Glick, 124–25
schools. *See* education
Seema (study participant), 65–66
self-esteem/self-confidence, 99, 134, 138
service sector workers: downward occupational mobility and, 49–50; increasing demand for, 8; intersectional framework and, 59; labor relations for, 75–76; men as, 92, 112; in Nepal, 33; socioeconomic status and, 143; work conditions for, 75–76
sewa (service), 122–23, 159

sex trafficking, 34, 34nn14–16
Shanti (study participant), 61–62
Sherpa communities, 86
Shree Krishna, 125, 160
Shyma (study participant), 135
single mothers, 91, 117
Smith, Dorothy, 6
social capital, 4–5, 8, 15, 39, 53
social class, 58–60, 82, 86–87. *See also* socioeconomic factors
socialization, 98, 112n9, 145
social media, 90
social movements, 26
social networks: autonomy and, 135–36; formation of, 139; informal work sector and, 47, 51–53, 53n4, 57, 60, 60n1, 64; for new migrants, 45, 83, 83n6; for recruiting replacement workers, 83, 83n6; of Vietnamese migrants, 128. *See also* transnational networks
social organizations: economic support for, 119–24, 138, 146–47; US-based Nepali, 129–33, 148. *See also* nongovernmental organizations (NGOs)
sociocultural events and practices: economic support for, 114, 125–29, 150; engagement with, 3, 137–38; importance of, 15, 128–29, 149; informal work sector and, 53–57; in labor relations, 80; pan-coethnic labor market and, 145; transnationalism and, 13–14. *See also* cultural capital; social networks
socioeconomic factors: downward occupational mobility and, 49–50; Indian employers and, 54; labor force participation and, 33–34; in labor market, 9; reasons for migration and, 31, 35–36n17, 37–41, 43–44, 45, 143; of

research participants, 155–57; study participants status and, 49, 49n2. *See also* middle-class status
Sony (study participant), 75
Southeast Asian employers, 20, 47. *See also* Indian employers; pan-coethnic labor market
Southeast Asian migrants: agency and activism of, 113; Das Gupta on, 11; definition of, 11n8, 71–72; informal work sector and, 9, 53–57; Purkayastha on, 14; similarities and differences with, 4. *See also* migration patterns; pan-coethnic labor market
Southwest region, 10
sponsors: for children, 89, 119, 120; decision making for, 110; empowerment and, 127; green cards and, 87, 97; Indian employers as, 78–79; public transportation and, 52. *See also* green cards
Sri Lanka/Sri Lankans, 11n8, 22, 29, 32, 89, 92
stealing accusations, 66–67, 144
stereotypes, of nationality, 68–69
structural factors: in choosing informal work sector, 46–47, 48–49, 57, 67–68; in gender roles, 111–12; in mothering, 88–89
structural inequalities, 24–25, 25n4, 26, 26n7
students, 2, 2n1, 31
St. Vincent migrants, 125
subsistence economy, household, 33
Syama (study participant): economic support by, 116–17; family life of, 94–96; reasons for migration and, 141, 142; social networks and, 51; on work conditions, 70–71, 74

Tamang, Seira, 86

Tara (study participant), 37–39, 45, 91, 98–99, 117–18

taxes, 48, 50, 51, 57, 75

teaching, 36n19, 38–39, 98

Teej festival, 108, 108n7, 126, 160

television, 56

temple construction, 124

Thailand, 30

Thakali communities, 86

Third World women, victimization of, 5, 10, 16n9

Tibetan-origin groups, 86

Tibeto-Burman ethnicity, 103

trade, free, 7, 25, 90

trafficking. *See* sex trafficking

transnational activism, 14–15, 16–17, 133–36, 139, 146–47, 148

transnationalism, 13–17, 113–39; agency and, 15–16n9, 15–17, 113, 129–33; community building and, 15–16, 113–39, 140; conjugal relationships and, 92–97, 105; definition of, 13; empowerment and, 13–17, 21, 112, 133–36, 147; engagement with, 2–3, 3n3, 4, 5; everyday lives and, 13, 21; family lives and, 87–88; gender roles and, 13, 15–17, 87–88; patriarchy and, 145–46; studies of, 13–15, 150; women as primary income earners and, 97–99

transnational mothering, 88–93, 91n2, 92n3, 111

transnational networks: economic support through, 120; engagement with, 148; informal work sector and, 47, 50–53, 53n4, 57; migration process and, 35–36, 38–39, 40, 41, 45, 141

transnational practices and activities, 114–15; agency and, 2–3, 124–29,

146–47, 148; autonomy and, 135–36; civic engagement and, 115–18, 129–33; eventual return to Nepal and, 136, 136n5; examples of, 116–18; for nonfamily members and social organizations, 119–24; percentage of income for, 115–16; types of, 115–18

Transnational Villagers (Levitt), 14–15

Tribhuvan Shah, 24

undocumented workers: informal work sector and, 50; "insider" status and, 19; legal migrants as, 4; mothers as, 90; pan-coethnic labor market and, 53; workplace rights for, 67

UNDP (United Nations Development Programme), 33

unemployment, 7, 29, 110

United Kingdom, 27–29, 30

United Nations Development Programme (UNDP), 33

United States Citizenship and Immigration Services (USCIS), 32, 32n13

Universal Declaration of Human Rights, 26

US-based Nepali social organizations, 129–33, 148

USCIS (United States Citizenship and Immigration Services), 32, 32n13

USCIS Yearbook 2003, 31

varna, 23, 160

Vietnamese, 109–10, 128

violence: political, 25, 26, 30, 31, 42, 85; against women, 11, 11n7, 99, 132; women's movement and, 85. *See also* abuse

visas: applying for, 8; Diversity Visa (DV) Program, 3n5, 32, 32n13, 43, 50; F1 Student, 6n6; F2, 2; informal work sector and, 50, 52; visitor, 88, 95
visitor visas, 88, 95

wage differentials, 1, 44, 98, 149–50
Wallerstein, Immanuel, 55
weekend work, exploitation of, 58, 61, 63, 66
When Women Come First: Gender and Class in Transnational Migration (George), 109
white employers. *See* American families
women migrants. *See* migrant women
women's movement, 26, 35, 85–86, 143
work conditions, 21, 60–68, 143–45; American families and, 79–80; for cashiers, 75; for childcare providers, 10–11, 58, 62–66, 74–75, 143–44; codependence and, 76–80; for domestic workers, 10–11, 75, 143–44; examples of, 61–67; lack of control over, 68; prejudice and, 70–72, 80–83; for restaurant workers, 73; for service sector workers, 75–76; structural factors in, 68. *See also* labor exploitation
work hours, 60–61, 61n2, 62, 63
work permits, 50, 63, 68. *See also* green cards
workplace rights, 10–11, 136–37, 137n7, 147–48
World Bank, 30–31, 34

Zinn, Maxine Baca, 19
Zontini, Elisabetta, 97, 105

Shobha Hamal Gurung is professor of sociology and women and gender studies at Southern Utah University. She is also the co-coordinator of SUU's Women and Gender Studies Minor Program and the program director of the Nepal Studies Program. Her areas of teaching and research include gender and labor; migration, immigration, and refugees; globalization, transnationalism, and diaspora; human trafficking; and social inequality, intersectionality, and human rights. Her current research project, in which she collaborates with Mary Romero, explores the sociocultural and emotional lives of Bhutanese refugees of Nepali origin in two US cities—Salt Lake and Seattle. Some of her notable publications include "Women Weavers in Nepal: Between Global Market and Local Craft Production" (2004); "Growing Up Hindu: Mapping the Memories of a Nepali Woman in the United States" (2008); "Nepali Female Migrants and Informalization of Domestic and Care Work: Service or Servitude?" (2010); "Gendered Labor: Experiences of Nepali Women within Pan-Ethnic Informal Labor Markets in Boston and New York" (coauthor, Bandana Purkayastha, 2013); "Sex Trafficking and the Sex Trade Industry: The Processes and Experiences of Nepali Women" (2014); "Shifting Gender Roles and Shifting Power Relations: Immigrant/Migrant Nepali Families in New York and Los Angeles" (2014); "Fluidity and Realities of Race, Class, and Gender: Different Places, Times, and Contexts" (2014); and "Dynamics and Ramifications of US Immigration and Visa Policies: Nepali Transnational Workers, Families, and Children in the United States" (2015).

She has received funding for her research projects from the School of Humanities and Social Sciences at Southern Utah University; the Institute for Asian American Studies at the University of Massachusetts–Boston; the Ford Foundation's Project on Low-Wage Work, Migration, and Gender; and the University of Illinois at Chicago. She has presented her scholarly work locally, nationally, and internationally for various communities—academic, activist, NGOs, and INGOs.